Rural Route One

William McDaniel McCollum

Once in a while, I find it is good to say "Yes" to things, even when I'm not entirely sure where that response will take me. Usually, the end results of those decisions have led to something good, and this case is no exception. My path intersected several times with the author of this book throughout the late winter and early spring of 2011, creating for me a professional journey through the world of editing and an emotional journey of reminiscence through stories and memories which have been all but lost to those of my generation.

The author's story is about a boy growing up on a rural route in the South, his many siblings, his parents, his small school and his military service. Yet, the real meaning of this book—what it's *really* about—lies in his descriptions of those basic emotions, expressions, and experiences that define us as human beings: love, acceptance, attitude and circumstances.

-T. Matteson Toenjes

To Conley,

of course

Chapter 1

A Day Late

The doctor was on the way. His black 1931 Ford was not a fast car, plus the one-lane dirt road had lots of ruts, and it was a rough ride. A few days back, March rains had turned the dusty country roads into a mess. He was hurrying and was running late. My mom's labor pains were three minutes apart, and she was worried. Death had visited their house twice. In December of 1939, dad's mom had passed away and, in March 1940, their firstborn only lived for a few hours. Now, just a little over a year later, in the same house and the same bed where I was conceived, she tried keeping herself calm. I was already a day late. My dad had a fire going in the kitchen cook stove; there needed to be plenty of hot water. Clean homemade towels were ready. My mom's mother "grandmother Vines" was on the way, and Mrs. Hendrix, the neighbor lady who lived about a mile down the road, had just arrived. She came in an old one-horse buggy with a basket of food, warm cornbread, canned pork, and banana pudding; she said that the doctor would be there soonly.

March in Alabama is a very good time to be born. Trees are budding; honeysuckles, wildflowers, lilacs, and the southern pines smell really good, and the aroma is intoxicating. Farmers at this time of the year are usually in the fields plowing and getting the soil ready to plant. The temperature was now around seventy degrees, and some of the farmers had already planted cotton. The window of opportunity for getting the soil ready to plant was short. Yet, it all stopped on that 28th day of March 1941 at 2:30 p.m. I am so pleased that it did, and I am and will be forever grateful. My mom said I came into the world kicking and crying, and that was a good sign. Later, as she was holding me close to her breast, I stopped crying and she swears that she saw my first smile.

My dad Gertis Stephanmeyer McCollum had a very good education, and was well read. He was six-feet-four and a very good basketball player. In his senior high school picture, he stands head and shoulders over the rest of his classmates. After graduation, he remained at home, helping his mom and dad on the farm; they were sharecroppers. They lived in Morgan County, Alabama, close to a small rural community called Gum Springs on a very dusty one-lane road. He was the third generation of sharecroppers—a very hard way to make a living—even back then. They farmed with mules and horses—with a one-bottom plow, a one-row planter, and a one-row cultivator. Of course, they picked cotton and corn by hand, and it was a full-time job keeping the weeds and grass from overtaking the crops. They never owned a tractor; some of the farming equipment belonged to the landlord. The farm consisted of fifteen acres of cotton, twelve acres of corn, ten acres of hay, and twenty-four acres of pasture. They had two milk cows, some chickens, and a couple of hogs. That was a large farm for two guys and two workhorses.

Not far from Gum Springs lived a Mrs. Lena Vines with her four daughters, Martha, Colleen, Lois, and Ruth, and three sons, Leroy, Leo, and Jessie. My mom, Martha Magdalene, was the oldest of the Vines girls. They were a very hard-working family. Each of the girls would have been a great pick for any fellow. It looks like my mom did the picking, as she really liked the guy across the field, who waved at her each time he passed their house.

Mom did not have much of an education. At eleven years old, she dropped out of the fifth grade. Dad was seven years older than she was. Here, I must say even though my mom had dropped out of school at a very young age, she was the one who read to me when I was a child. Later on, she was the only one who wrote letters to me, up until the very end of her life.

Granny Vines advised my mother never to marry a man, until she had seen him in bib overalls. If he looked good in overalls, he would look good—really good—in a suit. The Vines lived down a ways and across the road. My mom had seen my dad in overalls a number of times, since that was what most farmers wore during that time. He wore bib overalls for the rest of his life, and at the end, he was buried in them…at his request.

According to eyewitnesses, it was love at first sight for my mom. She said he looked handsome in bib overalls, and he thought she looked beautiful in her hand-stitched, faded dress with large blue flowers. Her auburn hair shone in the light and made her look even more beautiful to my dad. Grandma Vines has told me a number of times that she knew they were getting serious, since my mom was going to the mail box three or four times a day. Just about a year later, they showed up at the preacher's house —my dad in bib overalls and my mom in her best homemade dress, made by hand from four flour sacks. Fifteen minutes later, and minus two dollars, they were husband and wife. Did they talk it out and eventually make a decision, or did they just decide to get married and start up housekeeping and have lots of kids? Well…I am the oldest living of ten children; she was pregnant for a total of ninety months throughout her lifetime.

They honeymooned in the same house with my grandpa and grandma McCollum; that was the way it was, and it seemed to work out pretty darn good. The next day, the newlyweds were working side by side in the large garden out behind the house. Mom later told me that it was a wonderful day and the best garden she had ever seen.

Mom was a small lady about five-foot-five and never weighed more than one hundred thirty pounds. She was now twenty-one years old with a very sick baby. Granny Vines told me later that two days after I was born, I was not doing very well and that she and my mom did not think I was going to make it. Grandma Vines told my dad to go find a farmer who had a cow that had just had a calf and get some colostrum (the first milk after the calf is born). I believe that, after the first child, my mother's milk had dried, or maybe something had gone wrong, because she never nursed any of us. I am told my dad left in a run and later returned with almost a gallon of colostrum. Thanks to the Guernsey cow the farmer said was about two days early…the timing was right; it was a good thing I was a day late. A few months later, I developed rickets and almost died again, but I somehow made it. For the most part, I have never been sick again and I am very healthy to this day.

Everyone who knew my grandpa James D. McCollum and Grandma Winnie M. (Thompson) McCollum said they were really fun people to be around. They were always laughing and kidding each other. My grandpa was a great storyteller and loved telling all kinds of stories after supper at the kitchen table. They loved company; their house was always a welcome place to be; there was always plenty to eat and, usually, the best homemade pie ever. They were just plain county folks who were easy to please, fun to talk to and just hard working people.

My cousin Ruby still talks about the great times she had with them, that she dearly loved visiting their farm and it was always a fun time at their kitchen table. She still talks about how nicely she was treated as a little girl and how much she loved all the adventures on the farm. They were just easygoing people who loved the country way of life.

Most people who knew my grandpa called him "Uncle Jim." He never took himself very serious and always laughed at his own jokes. Grandmother McCollum died before I was born. Everything I have ever heard about her has been positive. She was a large lady, a good cook, and as gentle and sweet as any woman in the country. My father adored her. I am told that no one ever heard her utter a harsh word, and that my Grandfather treated her like a queen. Now, that makes me smile. Later while I was growing up he treated my mom the same way, he was the kindest man and so gentle with all of us kids. He was my hero.

I think folks back then lived at a much slower pace; they were always willing to help their neighbors. They depended on each other and were always there to lend a helping hand. This was the kind of world and family that I was born into there in that very rural setting on rural route one.

Where I grew up, dirt roads were the main highways. About every two or three miles was a farmstead, and most people farmed with mules and horses. Their living came from the land with lots of hard work. The roads were just one-lane and narrow; when you met your neighbor, you pulled over, stopped, and visited...that was a really good thing.

Chapter 2

THE UNPAINTED MANSION

It had been raining all day and now it was almost suppertime. There was a knock at our front door, and we wondered who in the world it could be. The fellow standing there on our front porch was covered with mud up to his knees. He said his car was stuck just down the road aways; he wanted to know if my dad would hitch up the team and pull him out. "Of course," dad said, and a short while later, the team was all ready and hitched to the steel-tired wagon. He threw a chain in the back, and I climbed in with them, since I wanted to watch the show. About a half-hour later, the fellow, his wife, and two kids were on their way. There was no charge for the tow service. About a week later the same guy stopped and left us a batch of homemade cookies. I was hoping that maybe he would get stuck again soonly..... The cookies were really good. The country roads were always a mess after a good rain...but not a problem if you had a couple of good workhorses. At this time in my life, I had never been on a paved road; all I knew was the dusty, sometimes muddy, dirt country roads there on Rural Route One, Joppa, Alabama.

The Old Crawford Place was about four miles from Ryan Cross Roads. This was as close as we ever came to living in a southern mansion. It was at the bottom of a very steep hill on a dirt road. Back then, it was called the Crawford Shoot, I believe, because it was such a steep and straight road from the top all the way down to the bottom. Coming down, you could really go fast, and most drivers did just that. It was like they were being shot down the hill. Mr. Dewitt Crawford, the landowner, would let his 1936 Chevrolet pickup truck coast down, without using the brakes, and you had better stay out of the way or be run over. Some said that it was a scary ride down with him, and yet he paid no attention to the looks on his riders' faces.

This is as far back as I can remember. I was about four years old, and everything was new, exciting, and interesting to me. The old Crawford place was a two-story unpainted house with two fireplaces. Looking at it from the front, the house had one fireplace all the way at the end at the left side and one all the way at the end on the right side. The front porch went all the way across the front of the house. There were a few cedar trees in front, twenty-five to thirty-five feet tall. All kinds of trees surrounded the house, and the driveway up to the house had trees on both sides. Inside the house, the walls and ceilings were made of planks ten inches wide, and this was unusual. I have never in my lifetime seen another house with planks that wide that have been used for the walls and ceilings. Even though it was old, it was in good shape, and it was very well built. The house was off the road on a small knoll about a quarter of a mile. There was not much traffic back then, yet when there was an occasional car, we could see it from our house. The driveway from the road to the house was the red clay type with no gravel. Of course we had no motor vehicle, but when those with vehicles used the driveway, it had to be dry or it was hardly passable.

By this time, I had a little brother and a baby sister, Conley who was born in 1942 and Lena Elizabeth born in 1943. I can remember so many things that happened here; it was a great place for Conley and me to explore...and to get into trouble. My mom would take us out into the woods to gather hickory nuts. The nuts were as big as walnuts. Later, Mom had jars of nuts for baking cookies and nut bread. There were lots and lots of hickory trees, and some were very large. I learned to love the outdoors while living there. We would lay the hickory nuts on a large rock and crack them with a hammer or a stone. Mom had a hard time keeping Conley and me from eating them as fast as we shelled them.

The barn was downhill and to the right of our house. It was a great place to hang out, to play and have fun. I still love barns; the old ones are the most fascinating. This one was even more special, because it had been built without any nails. I could not believe how well built and how strong it was. Wooden pegs held everything together. Some of the doors had wooden hinges, and some you had to slide to open and close. It was a large barn with five stables, a corncrib, and a feed-room area. The loft was the best place to play and hide out; the mommy cat always had her kittens there. This house and barn were very old, yet they were well built and, for sure, both had class.

We had two horses that were used for farming, both were large-framed workhorses named Nancy and Pearl. I remember Pearl giving my dad some problems. He got mad and started mistreating her. My mom was out in the front yard and saw what was going on, Right away she came to the horse's rescue; she was right in my dad's face. Boy was she mad; she was giving him a piece of her mind, pointing her finger at him. Mom would not tolerate any misuse of animals. She grabbed me my by the arm and walked back to the house so fast that I couldn't keep up, she was dragging me along the ground. I was old enough to have learned a valuable lesson; don't mess with my Mom. My dad was mad at the horse and now mad at her. I remember thinking about how much I liked that about her and loved that she would not let any of our animals be mistreated.

Dad could get mad and pout for days at a time, but she didn't really care. I think he could have pouted for weeks at a time, and it wouldn't affect her least bit. She was a redhead—a tough lady—and when she got mad, you got out of her way. Later, I found out that you better not mess with her kids, either. She would get fighting mad in a minute. I was so glad that she was my mom.

About fifty yards from the house, there was a small cave with a small stream of water flowing out of it. In the hot summer months, we kept the milk and butter there, since it was cool. We had no electricity, and before supper, Conley and I would be sent to the cave to get the milk and butter. One time, we took the long way around. We were playing, and Conley fell into a hole. That scared me almost to death. He was down there looking up at me crying, but I had to leave him down there while I ran back home, thinking that he was going to die in that hole. My grandpa, who was staying with us at that time, came to his rescue, and I was elated to see that he got him out and that my little brother was okay. Of course, mom was upset with me for leading him astray. That would not be the last time I got us in trouble.

There was one bed in the living room where dad slept; in the next room, mom slept with my baby sister. We did not have baby beds—ever. I can remember, later on, mom having two babies in her bed, sleeping with her at one time. One night, I heard my little sister crying, and my dad told my mom to stop that baby from crying, because he had to get some sleep, which was the dumbest thing ever for him to say to her. She replied in a clear and plain voice that, if he could do any better, he should come in and take her place. Of course, he never said another word. My mom was a smart lady.

One Sunday afternoon, a small plane was flying over our house; it came over every fifteen or twenty minutes, so dad, Conley, and I walked up the Crawford Shoot road to see what was going on. Conley told my mom if we found it that he would put it in his pocket and bring it back so she could see it. There in a farmer's pasture, I saw a yellow airplane, and it was the first time in my life I had ever been that close to such a thing. It was so big there on the ground. The pilot who, back then, was called a "barn stormer," charged a dollar for a ride. He was using the farmer's pasture for the runway. Dad was talking to the pilot, and then he picked up Conley and was going to let him go for a ride. I was scared to death that he might put him in the airplane. I could not stand the thought of him going up in that thing, as he might fall out. Conley and I were thinking the same thing. He was giving my dad a fit, and Conley and I were both thinking *let's get the heck out of here*. Then he picked me up and took me to the plane, and I was sure he was going to set me inside and let the pilot fly away with me in that thing. If Conley didn't want to go for a ride, I darn sure didn't. I was scared to death. My dad was a big man, but he was no match for me. I fought him all the way. I did not want to go near that airplane. Little did I know that, thirty years later, I would pay fifty dollars an hour to get my pilot's license learning how to fly a plane just like that. It was a Piper J-3 Cub, and today, I would give anything to own one. Back then, I was glad to see it fly away and not return to the pasture. Our dad was disappointed with us, but we didn't care. We were both just glad to have our feet on the ground.

Grandpa McCollum would come and stay with us for a while. We always liked that. He was the tallest man I had ever seen; at six-foot-six, he towered over everyone and everything. He was funny, liked to tease, and could tell some of the scariest stories that he swore were true. I remember him cutting wood with a double-bladed axe. I think I got a bit too close to him while he was working one time, and he set me down and gave me a lesson on how dangerous the double-bladed axe could be. He told me how easily I could get hurt. He said, "Little boy, don't you ever think about touching this axe," and gave me a stern look. Well, as you know, do not tell a young kid to *never* do something. A few days later, Conley and I were at the woodpile, and that axe was there. I couldn't help it; the axe was calling to me. I convinced Conley to hold a small piece of wood, and I was going to cut it to pieces. Conley got his fingers in the way—it was his own fault of course—and I almost cut one of them off. There was blood everywhere, I just knew he was going to bleed to death, and I knew for sure I was in the worst kind of trouble ever. Now, I don't need to write here what happened to me…it was not one of my better days. Conley survived, and his fingers healed. However, I will never forget how scared I was, and the stripes on my rear end were there for a long time, as a reminder. I also kept my distance from my grandpa for a long time.

When it really rained hard, we could stand in the kitchen door and see the water coming down off the mountain like a real, live waterfall. It was an awesome sight.

The house and barn is no longer there, and that's a shame. It was a great place for a mansion; the view looking across the pasture and the fields at any time of the year was a sight to see. The tall stately trees and the colors there in the valley and along the hillside were breathtaking. It was the best of times there on Rural Route One in Joppa, Alabama.

Chapter 3

Living In The White House

At about five years old I was now entering the most wonderful time of life when almost everything amazed me. All the wonders of life were coming alive—little things at that time I couldn't figure out, which caused me to ask hundreds and hundreds of questions. I think my dad got really sick and tired of me asking so many "how come" questions. He once told my mom, "That boy asks way too many questions." (I was called boy a lot back then) Life was so wonderful that I wanted to know everything all at once, and I haven't changed all that much over the years. I've been blessed with so much for so long that I don't ever want it to stop.

This was the only painted house we ever lived in, while I was growing up on Rural Route One, and it was painted white. Again, it was not far from Ryan Cross Roads—about two miles, mostly east. It was closer to Ryan than the Old Crawford Home, but it was still very country-like with dirt roads, small wooden bridges, and lots of trees just out our back door. It was a smaller house, and the only house we lived in that had no front porch. The barn was out back and downhill from the house. Just out front on the dirt road, an old wooden bridge made it possible to cross over a small stream that ran down through our pasture. I remember daydreaming about catching a really big fish, but this was all in my mind, of course, because there was hardly enough water for a tadpole or a frog in the stream. However, the whole scene of the house, pasture, woods, and stream were so beautiful, they could have enticed Norman Rockwell to bring his paint and brushes. This was a really fun place to live. I went back to see if the house was still there thirty years later and, sure enough, it was, but it had been moved across the road and was being used for storage. It was still pretty much the same.

I remember running through the pasture and across the road like a deer. There were neighbors close by, and we could see their house from where we lived. Living within sight of other houses half a mile down the road was considered very close back then. We could even see smoke coming from their chimney and see their livestock out in the pasture. I visited the neighbors a lot, and I know now that I showed up at their houses most of the time uninvited and therefore unexpected. I'm sure I was a pest most of the time, wanting to know about this and that.

Dad had taken a job at the Ryan School as a janitor. He was paid $40.00 per month; he worked a lot of hours for that small amount, but money was hard to come by then. He worked five days a week, plus the nights when there was a ball game. He still farmed while working at the school full time. My grandpa and my mom did a lot of the farm work.

One of our neighbors was Mr. A.C. Densmore, who lived not far from us; he would later become a Boy Scout leader. Mr. D was a no-nonsense type man with a very pretty and wonderful wife. He was always giving me a hard time. He had a dry sense of humor, but once he had fooled me, he would really laugh out loud. I really liked both of them. Since Mr. D was always trying to pull one on me, I thought turnaround was fair play. From time to time, when I walked past their mailbox, I would put a rock or a rotten apple in there, thinking they would never know who did it. Later, my dad gave me a good chewing out about that. I wondered how they knew it was me.

Another Densmore lived on the other side of us. Mr. Andy had a blacksmith shop about a half-mile down the road. Now, if you have never been in an old blacksmith shop, you are missing out on a very wonderful experience. Mr. Andy would make horseshoes for all the mules and horse's he also sharpen plow blades and other tools that the farmers used. It was fun to be there and see him work. Just being there with the smell of the fire, the hot metal, watching all the work going on, and listening to the farmers talk was very interesting for me, since I was so inquisitive and had lots of questions. Again, my dad would apologize, saying that I asked too many questions. The shop was just a shack with a front overhang. Mr. Andy had so much stuff there; everything had to be in the right place. I always wondered what all of those tools were used for. There was a hand-crank fan that would blow air on the hot coals when he turned the crank. I remember Mr. Andy letting me turn the crank, which blew air on the fire and caused the coals to turn red hot. Conley wanted to do the same; he was turning the crank and I thought he was getting too close and was going to get burned. I was trying to pull him away, but he resisted, and I almost caused him to fall. My pants got a warming from dad for being so stupid.

Mr. Andy would hold the plow point with iron tongs until it was red hot. Then he would take a large hammer and shape the point to make it sharp. He didn't use a grinder. I can still see it in my mind to this day. I never understood how he could take a very large horse or mule and get the shoes measured, fitted, and then nailed to the hoof without getting kicked around or hurt. Plus, how did all this not hurt the animal? I knew then that was a job I did not want.

Mr. Andy's wife was a great cook and had a very large garden. Each time I remember being there, she would give us something to eat. I thought she was the most wonderful lady, but not just because she gave me something to eat...well, maybe. Mrs. D made ketchup from scratch and gave us some to try; it was the first time that I had ever had something like that. It was so very good. It was the first time in my life I had tasted ketchup, and the last time I ever tasted it homemade.

There at Ryan, mom and dad went to the Little Vine Primitive Baptist Church where our dad served as the clerk for the church. He also had a very good voice for singing. During the year, the church and other Primitive Baptist churches would hold an all-day singing and he would take part in them; sometimes being gone for a couple of days. The singing was a very beautiful and unusual kind of singing; it was sung in a different key as others would sing them. I have been trying to get some recording of that kind of singing but haven't had any luck so far. I believe it is called the old-time Sacred Heart singing.

One time, a visiting preacher came and stayed at our house overnight. We had just gotten in the mail a box of fifty new baby chicks. The little chicks were in cardboard boxes, and we kept them in the house for the first few weeks. For me, the smell was pleasant, and they were so cute. It was something to see how little they were and see them grow. Anyway, the visiting preacher slept in the same room with the little chicks, and the following Sunday, as he was introduced at the church, he made a remark that, for the first time in his life, he had slept with the chickens. I think he meant for that to be funny and it probably was. My mom, however, did not see it that way and took offense at his remarks. We never again had a visiting preacher stay at our house.

We had a really nice dog named Jack that followed Conley everywhere. If we went someplace, the dog had to be tied up or he would follow us. This one summer day, on Sunday, we hitched the team up and went to church, just a normal kind of thing. We tied up the team, and all of us went inside. A while later, while everyone was singing, I looked over at Conley, and there was Jack the dog curled up under the pew. Conley was grinning from ear to ear; the dog was wagging his tale, and they both had that happy look on their faces. I thought that was so funny. He had gotten loose, come to church, and someone left the front church door half open, and there he was going to church with us. Mom did not think it was the least bit funny. She had a fit and she got up and marched us out the door…with Jack. She made both of us sit in the wagon with that darn dog until church was over. She told us we had better be quiet and informed us that, if that dog barked just one time, she would be back out and it would not be funny. On the way home, she was upset at dad for not making sure the dog was tied up. She said something about everyone there finding fleas on their clothes. Dad kept his mouth shut which was a very wise thing to do. I thought it was nice that Jack wanted to be with us, no matter where we were at—even in Church. (Of course Jack was Baptist)

Chapter 4

The Griffin Place

I watched the road grader go by and thought what a sight it was to see. It was a really big yellow machine making the dirt road smooth. I was sitting there along the side of the road just looking. The road grader went by, and then stopped. The man got out and asked me my name and where I lived. I told him my name and that I lived on Rural Route One. I pointed and said I lived there in that old house. He said his name was Jack. I thought that was funny, since our dog was named Jack.

The Griffin place was only about a mile north of Ryan. Even back then, it was an old house with a rusty roof, and it was just there in the middle of nowhere. Even at that young age, I didn't like it, because I thought we had moved down the ladder. I liked the painted house so much better. The Griffin house was very close to the gravel road, and the barn was across the road a few yards down and away from the house. There were many small pine trees across the road, so it was a great place to play.

Conley and I built forts from the pine straw and sticks and generally just had fun playing there. I was not getting any smarter as I got older, and again I got in trouble doing something stupid…really stupid. We took some matches without my mom knowing; or rather, I took them, but at about four years old, Conley thought it was a good idea, too. We wanted to see if we could start a little campfire in the middle of the small patch of trees, which was maybe about half an acre large. Now, I don't remember if dad was just looking for us or if he could smell or see the smoke, but he found us all right. Conley saw him first and started running, because he knew we were in trouble. He told on me, of course, and that was the last time we ever thought about building a fire in a pine thicket, ever—and I mean *ever*. It was quite painful for me to sit for a few days after that. I think this was the only time in my life that, after my dad gave me a whopping, mom took over and gave me another one. Isn't there a law against being punished twice for the same crime?

Looking back I know it was a very dangerous thing to do, and we could have been burned to death, knowing how fast green pines will catch fire. We were out in the middle; the heat would have consumed us in a hurry. I still haven't forgotten and never will. It makes me scared to think about it…even today.

My grandfather stayed with us more while we were living at the Griffin place, and for me that was a good thing. He was and had always been a farmer, and as long as he was able, he liked working in the fields, helping my dad. He was a great guy, and he always took the time to talk to me and show me how to do little things. I remember him showing me how to take a sweet gum branch and make a whistle, how to make a flip stock, and how to switch for water. He even made a tree swing for us. He always took Conley and me with him when he went to the store, and of course, we got cold drinks. They cost a nickel back then, and we called them "a cold drink." Today, we'd call it Coke, Pepsi, RC Cola, or whatever. Back then, it didn't matter. It was just a cold drink. He was always fun to be with. He would brag on us and let us both sit on his knees. He loved to talk, so while we were at the store, we would hear some really good stories, as he talked with other customers.

My sister, Lena Elizabeth, was still a little girl but was growing up fast. She was about three years old then. When we came back from the store, we had to bring her something, too. It was fun seeing how she acted. She was super excited, even over a stick of peppermint candy, and it was fun watching her look through all the items to find her treat. I would try to hide them so she would really have to look to find them. One time, she couldn't find the candy, and she lit into me, as if I had taken the treat and eaten it myself. Boy o' boy was she ready to fight me! I found it for her in a hurry.

The Griffin house was just about a mile from the school. It was also close to the country store at Ryan, which was a good thing. My first grade teacher was Mrs. Smith. She was a really wonderful teacher and a wonderful person. At that time, she was well into her fifties and was close to retiring, I think. I still have a class picture with her and all of the students in the first grade. It's the only class picture that was ever taken while I was in school. My second grade teacher was Mrs. Hawk, and she was very pretty, I remember telling her that I wanted to marry her. She hugged me and said that was nice, but she was already married and was expecting a baby about any time. Whoa, I didn't know that. I thought Mrs. Hawk was rich because she had four pairs of shoes, all in different colors. I also remember Conley wanting to go to school with me, he would stand by the road and wave at me as the bus drove away. Conley and I were always together, and I'm sure he didn't understand why he had to stay home.

The house never smelled good to me for some reason. I think the roof leaked and had never been cleaned. It smelled even more after my mom got a coal-oil cooking stove—what we now call kerosene. I could always smell the coal oil even when Mom was not cooking. I didn't like the smell of it and thought the food tasted funny. Dad would get that "you better start feeding your face" look, when I didn't want to eat what was on the table, and I think mom thought it was funny. This is the only time during my growing up that we had not used wood to cook and heat the house. Sometimes, my mom had a hard time getting the stove lit when she wanted to start a meal. I remember sitting at the kitchen table and my grandpa telling my mom to be very careful with lighting the stove, as it could explode and catch her and the house on fire. From then on, I was deathly afraid that something like this might happen and cause harm to her. For some reason, for the rest of my stay at home, I was forever thinking that they would all be hurt, and I could not stand the thought of that ever happening. This was a fear that has always stayed with me.

There were two beds in the living room—one dad slept in and mom the other. Most of the time, she had at least one baby sleeping with her. In fact, there were only two rooms that we could sleep in, so beds were put wherever there was a place for them. Mom did not make the beds as we do today. She thought that we'd just get right back in them, so why make them?

Back then in 1940's and 50's there were no throw-away diapers. I remember this was not always a pretty sight or smell. My mom used whatever she had for diapers and always washed them out by hand. In fact, she washed everything by hand. We would draw water by hand from the well, fill a big black pot in the backyard, and start a fire to boil the clothes. We washed with homemade lye soap most of the time and used a stick to get the clothes out of the hot water and rinse them in tubs of cold water. Then we had to wring them out by hand and hang them on a line to dry. Washday was usually on a Saturday morning because she had us to help her. Believe it or not, I liked washdays. I was in charge of filling the pot with water and keeping the fire going. I also liked the smell of the whole operation, and mom would brag on Conley and me for being such good help. In the winter, when it got really cold—like below freezing—we would bring in the clothes all frozen and hang them on chairs in the living room to dry. It would be at least five more years before we got a wringer-type washing machine, and we had no electricity.

Aunt Zora (dad's sister) and her husband, Uncle Hoyt, and their kids who lived in McMinnville, Tennessee, came to visit us while we lived at the Griffin house. That was the last time she ever came to our house, and I think it's also the last time she ever came back to Alabama. Uncle Hoyt, Conley, and I were sitting on the front porch. He asked what we did for fun. I said we built forts, and I asked if he wanted to see the one we built. He never used my name; he just called me "Cotton Top." Both Conley and I had white hair, until we started to school. We went out into the pine thicket and he admired the construction of the fort. He then said let's build a fire and just sit here and talk. Conley got up and ran back to the house, yelling that Uncle Hoyt was going to start a fire. He remembered the trouble we had got into earlier, and everyone thought it was funny. Of course, Uncle Hoyt was having fun with us. Conley did not want another whipping.

While they were there, we made homemade ice cream. I remember eating so much chocolate ice cream that it made me sick, and to this day, I am not crazy about chocolate ice cream. I like chocolate but not the ice cream. The iceman would come by once a week, delivering ice in fifty-pound blocks. He would grip the ice with the ice tongs, turn around, and carry it to the icebox on his back. He did it with such ease that it looked like anyone could do it. It didn't take much to impress me.

The second Sunday in August, the little church that we attended called The Little Vine Primitive Baptist Church would have a pot luck with table after table of good-looking and great-tasting food. There were all kinds of pies, cakes, and so much good stuff to eat. The first time I remember being there was something special and inviting. I thought I had died and gone to heaven. The picnic was outside under the trees, and the food was arranged on homemade tables. The rule was, if people didn't bring their own chairs, they had to sit on the ground...and we did.

Conley and I were always hungry; we went back for seconds and thirds. There on one of the tables was a pecan pie that really looked good, and Conley didn't take just one slice of pie; he took the whole pan. I thought that was a great idea, and I thought it would be a good thing to help him consume it. Heck, he couldn't have eaten the whole thing. Again, mom had a fit, and I thought she was going to whip both of us in front of all the church people.

We would walk to church most Sundays, but when we had to take things with us to the picnic, we rode to church in a steel-tired farm wagon. The team of horses would be tied up in a special parking area.

Most folks had cars, but there were still a number of teams there. We could take our time eating, because the event lasted for hours. The southern women really do know how to cook and bake. I always looked forward to this event. We went to this church for about three years, but then my parents just stopped going. The first Christmas I can remember happened while we were there. Conley and I got a little red wagon, and we shared it for the most part. Conley would ride, while I pulled, and sometimes I would push while he would guide it. We were rough with it, and I don't believe it lasted very long. Perhaps we had a little too much fun with it.

Chapter 5

Ryan Crossroads

This little area was just a small place along the farm and market blacktop road, yet it was the lifeline for all the folks that lived in that area. Here is where I had my first soda pop, my first ice cream cone—that is, if I had a nickel. Also, if I was lucky enough to find five empty bottles, I could cash them in for a free pop.

Ryan Crossroads is where two roads cross: one a gravel road, the other a two-lane blacktop road. Highway 67 came right by the country store and was the main road to Decatur, the county seat of Morgan County. This was it, just a country store, two baptism churches, and the school.

The school was only twelve grades, with no preschool or kindergarten. The elementary school was first grade through the sixth grade in a five-room building with a U-shaped hallway through the whole building. The third and fourth grades were taught by one teacher at the same time. Each room had a coatroom and a stove to keep us warm in the wintertime. Black coal was used to keep the fire going. From time to time, the teacher would stop what she was doing to put more coal in the stove. I always thought it was a really neat setup. I liked the smell, the wooden floors, the way each teacher decorated her room. It was my school and I loved it.

There were no bathrooms inside, no indoor plumbing; it was all outside. One restroom for the boys and one for the girls was as far as I can remember. It was the normal thing, and most of us did not mind, because that was just the way it was back then. This was a real country school with some very wonderful teachers.

The high school was across the school grounds and was a completely different set up. We called grades one through six grammar school and seven through twelve high school. High school was much more modern with inside bathrooms and a nice gymnasium, a workshop, home economics room, and a large study hall. A coal furnace was used to make steam heat for the whole building. Mr. Randolph Ryan was the principal and I believe one of the best in the county. He was a strict, no nonsense type teacher. He was a great coach, teacher, counselor, principal, and judge and jury all at the same time. If you were sent to his office for something you did wrong, you would leave with your bottom a little bit warmer.

The school, store, and both churches were close together; all in the same area and on a gravel road.

The country store had just about everything you needed back then. It was a wonderful place to spend time. I remember flour being in cloth sacks and was stacked at least waist high. There were different color sacks and patterns. My mom would tell us what color to get, as she would use them for pillow cases, and she made shirts and dresses out of them by hand. She had no sewing machine. The store was full of all the things that were needed, and even more. There was only a small path to get around and look for what you wanted to buy. A coal-burning stove stood in the middle for heat in the wintertime. Farmers and customers would gather around it to keep warm, play checkers, talk, and just visit. There was a gas pump outside. You had to crank the gas up into a tank, which you could see. If you wanted five gallons there was a mark on the glass tank where you could see the five-gallon mark. I think the name on the pump said Pan-Am. I remember the gas being 19.9 cents per gallon.

The store for the most part always had customers, since it was the only store around that area. Mr. Jake Walker was the storeowner. He and his wife Mrs. Dorothy were great people and my dad thought the world of them. (Later, he would sell that store and buy the one in Hulaco, which is another story that will follow.)

Credit was extended to those who always paid their debts. Mr. Jake would write it down in his book and keep a running total of what you owed. I had permission to charge only five cents—no more—and could charge no more until those five cents was paid. He treated everyone the same. He allowed everyone so much credit, and if you did not pay, that was it, no more credit until the debt was paid off.

I remember a farmer...I won't mention his name here...but we knew him. He needed a few items of food for his family, and Mr. Jake would not or could not let him have anything, since he was way behind on paying his bill. Dad asked how much he still had on his credit. He allowed this man to use the remaining portion of his credit. I thought that was something. The fellow later came to our house with two laying hens and gave them to us. Debt paid in full.

So many wonderful memories were made here; it was a great thing to be there on a Saturday afternoon with all the farmers talking about the boll weevil, cotton prices, and of course, a lot of gossip.

The Little Vine Primitive Baptist Church and the Missionary Baptist Church were just behind the store. A gravel road ran between each church. The difference between these two churches was like night and day then—and it still is to this day. Church at Little Vine was on the second and forth Sundays, since the preacher had to go to another church on the first and third Sundays. Little Vine had foot washing, I think, once or twice a year, back then, and I think they still do. That little church was a neat place; it was like time had not advanced over the years.

No musical instruments were allowed, and there was no Sunday School—just good old fashion church preaching. The preacher was called by God to preach the gospel. I can remember some really good sermons preached there. A hat was on a small table, as you left the church. The preacher's pay was what was in the hat when the doors closed. This little one-room church standing back in a grove of trees was a sight to see and was one of the first buildings on the gravel road in that small community. It is still there and is a treasure for sure.

Conley and I visited the Missionary Baptist Church across the road a few times, but we thought the folks there did not appreciate us coming to church, since we were barefooted and wore our old, patched, blue work jeans or at least that is how we felt.

Just down the road from the store, Mr. Jimmy and Mrs. May Moon had a gristmill. They were the very best of people. Both were good and kind to all of us kids. We would take corn there to be ground into feed for the cattle, and the same corn to be stone ground into corn meal to make corn bread for us to eat. It made the best cornbread ever. The charge for all this was taken from a portion of the corn. You needed no money. It was something special to be there and watch the big round stone wheel turning, as it made our corn meal. I always like the smell and sound of this gristmill, and Mr. Jimmy always had a smile and a kind word for everyone—always.

So this was pretty much Ryan Crossroads. Just where two roads cross. I do not think Highway 67 was paved until the first part of the '50's. Until then, it was just two gravel roads that crossed at the store. A few houses were close by, maybe ten or twelve at the most at that time, and not many more now. This is where my grandparents lived and started their families, both the McCollum's and the Thompsons. I have read the late 1800s' census report of both families. Lots of history on our side came from this little area known as "Ryan Crossroads." This was a large part of our world back then.

Chapter 6

Moving To The Hollow

Change is almost always a wonderful and exciting thing. Moving to a new area, living in a different house, and getting settled was, for me, like starting a new life. We were surrounded by hills covered with trees and had fields of cotton and corn right out the back door. This was country living at its best, there on Rural Route One. We moved here in 1948 I was now about seven years old this is where I started growing up, becoming a young man, and learning the lessons of life.

So many things come to my mind, now, after both my parents have passed away, that I wish I would have talked to them about: Why did we move so often in my early years? Why did we not try to better our lot each time we moved? There are maybe a hundred other questions. This was or could have been a really beautiful area for a nice home, but we did not move up in the world, here in the hollow; we now lived in a sad looking house. I now know it's not the kind of house you live in that makes a family—but come on. We all want (or at least I do) a nice house to live in—nothing fancy, just a nice house. I wanted my mom to have a house she could be proud of, and I wanted one, too. I don't think I'm being selfish. Maybe we had no other choice at the time. Maybe that was all there was available. I don't know. All I know is that this was a big, old, ugly house.

Our house now was bigger but not better, but it was still our home. Let me tell you a bit about this big old house. When you came into the house from the front porch, you entered a fairly large, wide hallway that ran all the way through the house. A door to the right led into the living room, and over that door, an old double-barreled shotgun rested on two wooden, homemade forks. This was a large room; there was a big fireplace on the far wall. There were also two beds, a table for a water bucket, and an old trunk. We had no couch and no easy chair, only one rocking chair, and we had to bring a chair from around the kitchen table if we wanted something to sit on. The fireplace in the living room was made of field rock. Next to the living room, there was a large kitchen with a very unique wood-burning stove. It had a warming oven, a hot water tank, and a large baking oven. The eating table was in the middle of the room. Nailed on the wall were a few homemade cabinets made out of apple crates, and a fifty-pound flour barrel. Later, when we got electricity, the kitchen had a small white refrigerator.

There were two more rooms at the end of the hallway that we used: one to keep salted meat in, later to become a bedroom, the other one as a washroom. Later, the wringer-washer would be there with a table to put clean cloths on. My mom didn't like to iron, so when we needed something, we would have to go look through all the items to find what we were looking for. If we wanted it ironed we had to iron it ourselves, which was okay with me. We had two old heavy irons that we would have to set on the stove to get them hot. We would iron for a while, then put it back on the stove and use the other one. It worked pretty well. I had made a bench out of old planks for us to sit on while eating in the kitchen, and I used this to iron my clothes on. I would pull it over by the stove, get the iron hot, and get down on my knees and put a sharp crease in my pants. I would also roll my shirtsleeve up at least one time and iron a crease in that…I wanted to be in style.

Now, back to the old house. The house itself had never had a coat of paint on it. The foundation that held the house off the ground was of plain, old, field rocks, stacked on top of each other at different locations around the house. I often wondered what would happen if one of the rocks came off. Would the house fall down or tilt over?

We could see through the walls in some places in the house. It was a cold old house during the winter months. The water bucket would freeze, and the syrup would have to be set on the cook stove to be warmed up.

There was a chicken house out back and, behind that was the outhouse. It was not a good place to go during the hot summer days... believe me.

Being poor and living in a shack is not what I'm talking about here. No matter what, I think people should try to improve their lot, even with small things or in small ways.

For me, being poor was an asset in the long run. Heck, I didn't even know I was poor then. I figured I was pretty much about the same as other folks. I learned about life, work, money, getting along with what you had, being good neighbors and those were very valuable lessons. I think they might be more valuable than anything else I have ever learned. Now, if I'm poor, that's okay; I can deal with that, but I need to see the light at the end. Somehow, I need to find a way to work myself out of that situation.

The wonderful thing about moving to the hollow, we were surrounded by the very best of neighbors. Mr. John Ellenburg and his wife Mrs. Louie lived south of us. Their son John Jr. was my best friend, we called him (Pete). Father up the road Mr. General Bolding and his wife were just great people. Across the creek and down the road the Flacks lived; Mrs. Pauline Flack was my mom's best friend. There were a number of Densmores who all lived within a mile or so of us. All of them were the best of neighbors and they all married pretty ladies.... now that says a lot about those guys for sure. Mr. Oval Light and his family lived about a mile over the hill and was our insurance man. He was the best dressed man that I had ever seen and he also had a great personality. I wanted to be like him and look like him when I grew up.

Really, as I count my blessings, I don't have anything to complain about. There on Rural Route One in the hollow, still living on a dusty dirt road, life was pretty darn good.

I was still just a kid, now about eight years old, but I was growing up fast. I was trusted with the mules, and I could plow. I knew how to harness the team, and I knew "gee" from "haw." For the most part, I wanted to learn as much as I could, and I loved to work…I really did. Of course, I also wanted to play, but working kept me busy, and we had plenty of chores.

The Hollow was really out in the country. It was about two or three miles from Ryan and about the same distance from Hulaco. This was a beautiful location, surrounded by trees, and a nice-sized creek ran through the pasture nearby. It was a wonderful place to swim and take a bath in during the hot days of summer. There were all kinds of trees, including oaks, pine, poplar, sweet gum, hickory, and so many more all around us. It was such a sight to see when the trees turned so many different colors in the fall, and it was right outside our back door. The house itself was old and unkempt, but it was our home. Here, I grew up with so many memories. There was a drilled well out in the front yard, and it was deep; we had to work to get a bucket of water. We got a good workout on washdays and on days when the creek went dry, since we had to draw water for the livestock.

Conley and I had the job of keeping plenty of wood for my mom to use, and we also cut and split wood for heating. This was a constant chore for us, and it all had to be done just about every day, by hand, using a crosscut handsaw. By now, I was in trusted with the axe. I learned from my grandpa how to sharpen the crosscut saw and also how to set and shape the teeth so that it would cut nice and clean. Conley would always make sure that I had it "good 'n; sharp," as he would say, and he did not like to cut wood with a dull saw or axe. There was a special kind of tool that was used to set the saw…I wonder where it is now…

We were growing up fast and now had many chores to do. There was always plenty of work that had to be completed every day. Everything was done by hand, and it was a slow process, as one might expect. I believe everyone who lived in that area was pretty much in the same boat.

The barn was directly across the road with a pasture surrounding it. There were five stables for the animals, a corncrib, and a loft that was as big as the barn. A shed was on one side, and there we stored some of the farm equipment and the farm wagon. The barn was just a plain old barn, and it was very cold in the wintertime. I felt sorry for the animals there...and for the two boys who had to milk the cows.

The school bus stopped about a hundred yards from the house. We had to walk out to the Y-intersection to get on. The driver would blow the horn, as he came down the hill and across the bridge, and we would hurry out to get on. In the summertime, it wasn't bad, but during the winter, we stayed by the fire until we heard the horn; then we would head out on the run.

I was not a good student, I am sorry to say. I had to work hard to get a B, but most of the time it was a C. My mom and dad did not encourage any of us, as I remember, though I am sure they did not want us to fail. I think that working on the farm was just about as important as the school grades. Back then, we went barefoot to elementary school during the summer months. There were no inside bathrooms at the elementary school. There was a "four-seater" outside, built for boys and the same for girls. I didn't see this as unusual. That was just the way it was, and it was pretty much clean.

The fourth and fifth grades were taught in the same room by one teacher. It worked out pretty well. The elementary school teachers were Mrs. Mertis Smith, Mrs. Hawk (later Mrs. Childers), Ms. Mary Smith, Mrs. McGee, and Ms. Humphreys. Ms. Mary Smith (who was the daughter of our first grade teacher) taught the fourth and fifth grades at the same time.

Back then, the teacher was the law, the judge, and the jury, and you dared not get out of line very far. I am a first-hand witness to the punishment that could be handed out...and on more than one occasion. When I was in the third grade, three other boys and I were in the boys' restroom. We were having a peeing contest to see who could pee the farthest. I am sure we were loud and maybe using language that was not appropriate. We were having a good ole time and, all at once, Mrs. Childers appeared right there in the middle of us. She had come right into the boys' restroom and commenced slapping us upside the head. I couldn't believe that she would come right into the boys' restroom, but she meant business. She was rough with us, working all of us over with a number of heavy slaps to the sides of our heads. All of us were trying to get everything put away; we couldn't get out of there fast enough. I think a few of us peed on each other trying to get away from her, but we got the heck out of there for sure.

I could never look Mrs. Childers in the eye ever again without thinking she could still see me there in the restroom during that contest.

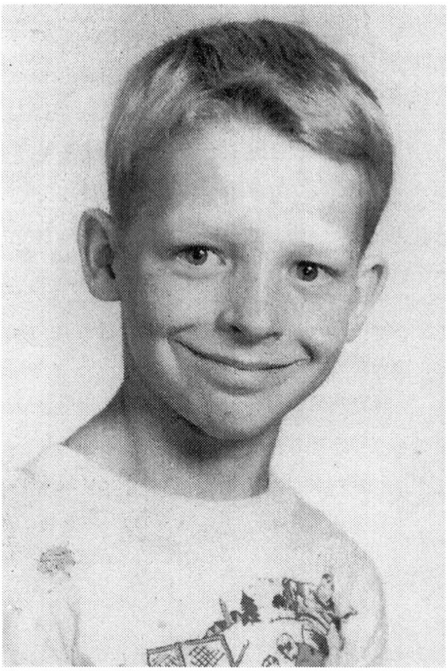

Little Will

Chapter 7

Growing Up

Farm boys and girls are always busy with so much to do and a lot of chores to be completed each day, but working is good for a person in so many different ways. All the work we did on the farm was accomplished without any kind of motorized tools. We cut wood with a crosscut saw, and we hoed cotton and corn...with just a hoe, of course. All this manual labor built muscle and kept us lean. There weren't many scraps left after a meal either. We ate everything that was put in front of us: cornbread and beans, and all kinds of garden food. Back then, there were no welfare programs; if you did not work, you did not eat, which is still a great idea in my opinion. With all that being said, life was good, and we had fun. We were surrounded by woods, creeks, and dusty country roads that led to other dusty roads. We went swimming in the creeks when we could find one deep enough. All we had to do was throw a rock in to scare the snakes away before we jumped in. There were many trails to explore, mountains to climb, and what a sight it was after we worked our way to the top.

As we were getting older, we had more responsibility. We were doing more and more of the farming. In the spring, we had cotton and corn to plant and then hoe, cultivating the crops one row at a time. Today, most farmers use a twelve-row cultivator and some even larger. The old boll weevil was a real pest and could destroy the cotton crop as it was maturing. That pesky thing had to be killed, or we would have no cotton to pick and then no money or food. We put a stop to that critter by using DDT. We used a contraption made of aluminum, which looked like a bucket and a duster, which weighed about ten or twelve pounds when it was full. The duster had straps, which mounted it around the chest, and the dust came out when we turned a crank as we walked down the middle of the rows, blowing all that chemical dust on the cotton plants. We were supposed to wear masks to keep from breathing the DDT, but it made it so hard to catch our breath. This was a very hard task, walking down the rows during the hot days of July and August, around a hundred degrees or more.

We had a lot to do during the summer months cutting hay, loading it by hand on the wagon, transporting it to the barn, throwing it up there by hand, and then working in the loft where it was even hotter. In the fall, we had to pick cotton. We had to pull a six- or seven-foot pick sack, bending over or crawling on our knees. No matter how we tried to complete the task, it was hard work. We also picked corn by hand, throwing it in the wagon and scooping it into the crib. Our large garden had a turnip patch, a pea patch, and cane to make sorghum syrup, so that required a lot of attention, too. Lena Elizabeth and Francis were able to help by now, and Mom would help in the fields in the afternoon. We had to make sure that all the fences were taken care of, which meant digging postholes and always making repairs. Digging the postholes by hand was very hard and slow work.

On the farm, there were cows, mules, horses, hogs, chickens, and a number of other animals, all requiring attention. Plus, there was *always* wood to cut and more so in cold weather. It had to be old, dry wood, since green, wet wood didn't work and would not burn very well in the cook stove. I can remember my mom saying, "Don't bring that new wood in here, if you want any supper." Conley would balk if he saw that an axe was not sharp, so I always tried to keep them sharp, or I would be the only one cutting. Even with all the work to be done, I did not feel that I was over worked. Conley and I had the energy…and we just did it.

Our dad was still working at the school, and he was a part-time carpenter, working during the summer months here and there. He also helped Mr. Dewitt at times. I remember them bailing hay with the old wire baler and an M. Farmall tractor. Later, it became a Super M. That was a messy job. I helped a few times, but the bails weighed almost as much as I did. I also remember the wooden kegs that we put water in to drink. You don't see those anymore.

Dad also worked at a sawmill not too far from where we lived. Back then, they would set up the mill and everything else close to where they were logging. He was the edger—the best edger in the county—and worked close to the big round blade that cut the tree into lumber. It was a dangerous job; if something went wrong, the edger was the one most likely to get hurt, since he was close to the blade and stood in the very middle of the whole works. A lot of men were mangled, and some were killed, while working around those primitive mills. I remember Dad coming home late in the afternoon with all of his clothes completely wet from sweat. I think he made five dollars working a ten-hour day from sunup to sundown. He needed the money because, by now, there were more mouths to feed: Conley, Lena Elizabeth, Francis, Wanda, Thomas Randolph, and me. That was six kids with three more yet to arrive.

Money was hard to come by. Dad was working for five dollars a day, and Conley and I worked for two dollars if we could find anything. We would cut sprouts in Mr. Dewitt Crawford's pasture and pick cotton for a dollar per hundred. Once, during the summer, we dug a storm pit for a fellow. We worked with a pick and shovel for a few hours a day for at least a week. When we were almost finished, the fellow said he didn't like where it was and that it was our fault. We didn't get one dime for all that hot, hard work. That was the last time we worked for him.

My mom kept busy, as well. She canned as much from the garden as she could. Working in the hot kitchen was not a pretty job, so we all helped get everything ready for her. Plus, she fixed three meals each day for all of us. We all pitched in to help mom because she had her hands full most of the time. I could go on and on about how hard my mom worked, and I never heard her complain once.

By now, there was not enough room at the kitchen table, and that was a problem only a 4x8 sheet of plywood could solve. It looked so big there, but it was just what we needed. Every year we would get a new oilcloth for the table. That was a nice thing because it smelled good, and it would be a different color each year. It looked so very fancy and made the kitchen look good. Getting a new cloth was very special for me, because it looked good sitting in our plain kitchen. Conley and I always sat on the same side of the table, and in the early years, we sat side by side. We had to be separated later on, though I need not explain why. I'll let you guess whose fault that was.

Later, we moved up in the world, because we had a big power line pole in our yard, which meant we had electricity. We had one light in each room hanging from the ceiling and one plug-in, plus a small refrigerator in the kitchen *and* a washer with a wringer. Conley and I watched it work and we both thought it was amazing. It was still quite easy to impress us. We had definitely moved up, but I had a slight problem with all this new stuff. When the wringer-washer was delivered, the man said for my mom and sisters to be careful. He showed her how it worked, telling her how easily someone could get an arm caught in the wringer. He also said that one lady had leaned over and somehow got her hair caught. I started thinking he could just take the thing back. Here, again, it really upset me having this stuff around because I didn't want my mom or little sisters getting hurt. This electric thing was not for me, since it really could be dangerous. I still liked the old battery-powered radio better, even if we could only listen for about an hour each night. Conley liked a different radio program, and he and I would get into it over which station to listen to.

Times were certainly changing. The world was coming to our front door, now, with things like radio and later T V. There were new things like cars, trucks, and tractors, and I was coming of age. What a wonderful time it was to be alive. I had now learned if I was ever going to get anywhere in life, it was up to me. I knew where I wanted to go, but I didn't know how to get there. School became hard for me, but I believed I had it in me to be a better student. I aimed to improve my grades even from a C to a B. It was only one step up, but it was so important to me that I get good grades. At times, I thought I was dumb kid, and then there were times I knew I was just as smart as anyone else. I just needed someone or something to encourage me. Back then, we called anything higher than the seventh grade "high school." The high school building was just across from the playground, and, as I looked across at that old stone building, I started to think about the future.

For the most part, I have always liked the teaching profession. Good teachers are worth their weight in gold. We had some good teachers and some that were not so good, which is pretty much like most schools. I don't know how much they were paid back then, but I would guess it is like today—they were not paid nearly what they were worth. I respected them and liked them, because they were good teachers, as far as I was concerned. Generally, if I needed help or didn't get it as fast as the others, my teachers would spend a little extra time with me. However, they only helped me if I put out the effort, and sometimes, that was a hard thing to do.

In the sixth grade, I was having problems with fractions. For some darn reason, I was just not getting math, and I was still having problems with diagramming a sentence. If I passed the next year, I would be moving across the schoolyard to the big building. I had to know about this math and English thing, because I was told that things moved faster in high school, and this was my last chance. Ms. Humphreys was an old maid and a no-nonsense lady. One day, as I was leaving her room, I hinted to her that I needed a bit more help and that I was trying to get a B from her on my report card. I asked if she would stay a little while after school to help me, and she promptly replied, "No."

The next day or so, we all went out for recess to play softball. I loved that game. We would team up and have some really good games. That day, Ms. Humphreys grabbed me as I ran out the door.

She said she had time to help me now. Gosh, I didn't want to miss the ball game. I was even playing first base that day, but she had that look that said "little boy, you better take advantage of this now", and I knew that I had to give up something to get something. I believed I learned more during those times than I learned during the whole class. Ms. Humphreys was a different person when just she and I sat down together. We spent a number of weeks going over all that stuff until it made sense to me. I also learned to value the teacher's time. Sometimes, she would call on me to go to the board and figure out a problem. This was a scary thing for me, but with time, I knew how all that worked. Then she would give me a word of praise, and then I would be on cloud nine. Ms. Humphreys was a great teacher, and I was going to miss her, as I left the elementary side of the yard. Finally, the last day of school came, and report cards were handed out to everyone as they left…accept me.

Ms. Humphreys said she wanted to see me before I left. I was beside myself: upset, scared, and the other students looked at me like they knew I had failed. That was really upsetting. After everyone left, the room was quiet, and it was just Ms. Humphreys and me. She pulled up a chair and told me to sit down. I was worried, but she had a pleasant look on her face, which was somewhat reassuring. She said she only had a few things to share with me; first, I was smart enough to get whatever grade I wanted to get and not to ever let anyone tell me any different. She also said that I was smarter than I thought I was. She made me feel very good with those words. It was my first pep talk. Then Ms. Humphrey's looked right at me with those dark, unblinking eyes and said, "William, if you want something bad enough, work hard enough to get it. You only have to put your mind to it." I wanted to hug her, but I left on the run, since I did not want to miss the bus.

Conley sat with me on the bus ride home and said, "You failed the sixth grade, didn't you?" I showed him the card, and he hit me on the shoulder, saying, "All B's!"

With a smile, I said, "Buddy Boy, I am on my way to high school!"

I still have that report card today.

I left that side of the school yard with a lot of good memories: learning to read with mom's help, exchanging cards with everyone on Valentine's day and small gifts at Christmas, school plays, singing "Happy Birthday," riding the bus, getting hit in the head with a baseball bat (I recovered), a few fights—some I won and some I lost, making friends that still last to this day, and most of all, learning something new every day. I wanted to know everything. Still, today, I remember—and always will—those days in grade school. I grew up there, and life was sooooo good.

at her, but I did. I did not see a smile...never seen a cow smile before... do cows smile?

Finally back home, I let her go out into the barn yard; the other cow was happy to see her back, and they started the same dang thing, jumping up and down smelling one another. I wonder if maybe they were smiling. I got back down to the woodpile and worked around there for a while. Conley came out and wanted me to tell him what happened. I said nothing happened. He said, "I wanna know." I said, "No, you don't want to know." He said, "Yeah I do" and I said, "No, you don't." We went back and forth, and he got up close to me and gave me a push and got that look in his eyes like he thought it was a secret I was keeping from him. He just had to know. So I said, "From now on, you're the one who takes the cows for a walk...'cause I was the oldest and that was not my job. Mom called us in for supper, and I was not a very talkative kid, since I thought everyone was looking at me with a silly smile. My grandpa...my buddy put his big ole hand on my shoulder and gave me a friendly pat. Life on the farm and all the adventures is something every growing boy—and girl—should be witness to. One thing for sure, I was glad that day was over.

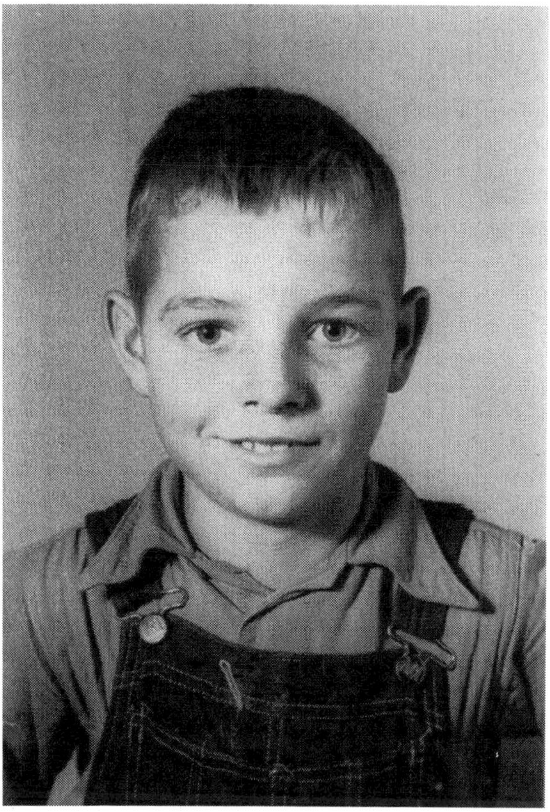

Conley

Chapter 9

Still Growing

Summers are pretty darn hot in the heart of Dixie—at times over a hundred degrees. For most of us, the less you wore, the better it was, and that included shoes. By the end of summer, when we really needed to be wearing shoes, our feet were tough; gravel, biers, sticks, and whatever we encountered was not a problem. Then, when cold weather came, we had to break in new pairs of shoes, which was not a fun thing to do for the first few days. All of us went barefoot, as long as we could, and for us, that was a good thing.

Here came the first day of high school, and was I excited. For me, it was kind of like how some folks feel going off to college. I had a new pair of blue jeans, pressed with a sharp crease (only in the front and rolled up one small roll), and a brand new boughten cotton short-sleeve shirt ironed with each sleeve rolled up and ironed. I felt good. My hair was combed, and by now, I was—with the help of Red Rose Hair Oil—getting control of that darned cowlick. My face was clean, and I smelled like lifebuoy soap, which I've always liked. My little sister Francis said I looked good, and if she said that, then I looked good.

Soon the school bus arrived, and it was good to be off on a new adventure. It was good to see some of my schoolmates, and there was one new student in my grade that had moved here from the great state of Tennessee. I was all smiles, since this was very different than elementary school—a much larger building, a gym, indoor plumbing, bathrooms, showers, and a study hall. This was big time.

Just one little thing messed up my first day. As all of us were going to what we called the "homeroom," I noticed that I was the only one not wearing shoes. Everyone else had on summer shoes and socks, and by now, others had noticed, and some were giving me that *look* and a snicker. My day was not going as well as I had planned. I couldn't believe it. I started asking myself a lot of questions: *Why did I not anticipate this? Why was I not paying attention to the trend? Why did I not see the students last year all wearing shoes? Why did our Mom and Dad not know that people in high school wore shoes?* I felt that someone should have told me to wear shoes to high school, but I had no one to blame but me, and I was beside myself. I could not believe that I was the only one without shoes. I felt so out of place. It pretty much messed up the whole day and the first part of this great adventure into the building of higher learning.

I could not wait until that first day was over. I had a pair of work shoes that were by now almost too small for me, but they would have to do until later. I cleaned them up and polished them with waterproof oil. They looked a bit tacky with my new blue jeans, but that was the best I had. Conley was still going barefoot to elementary school and thought it was funny that I had to wear shoes to school, because it wasn't cold yet. We never wore shoes, until it got cold outside. Later, I made sure he did not have to go through what I did on that first day.

High school was a different world for me, and I was really excited to have passed on to the seventh grade. I felt like a young man, no longer in grade school, yet in 1953 I was still just a kid at twelve years old going on thirteen. Here I was trying to create an identity. I wanted to be me. I was beginning to figure out who I was and what I wanted to be in life, but as we all know, it gets harder as you progress up the ladder. At least that was the case for me. In some ways, though, I was still a dumb kid doing some stupid, dumb things.

Usually, we would get all ready for school and mosey out to the fork in the road by the mailbox, where we all gathered to wait for the school bus. One time, while we were waiting for the school bus, some of us were horsing around, and I was practicing my baseball throw. I was throwing rocks at our mailbox, which we did often. This mailbox was in sad shape, anyway. It was one of those old boxes made from hard steel, and it had seen better days, for sure. We were all cleaned up and ready for school; two of my sisters, Francis, and Lena Elizabeth were looking good. Francis had her pretty auburn hair fixed up, and she wore a very pretty dress. Some of our neighbors who lived about a mile from us were there too. At about twenty feet away, I was pretty much on target; I could hit the mailbox, almost with every throw. We were just talking and having fun.

Our dad just happened to be working with the mules in the cotton field, just across the road. He noticed me doing this and told me to stop it, because I might hit someone, so I stopped…until he was far across the field. *One more throw and that will be it*, I told myself. I walked back a few more feet, eyed the target, leaned forward, then back, turned my head sideways to check the runner on first, and then let it rip. The rock was right on target and made a big bang as it rattled the mailbox, but this time, the rock bounced off and hit my sister Lena Elizabeth. She was bleeding. It hurt her, and she was really crying. My heart almost stopped beating; I had hurt my little sister. I cannot tell you how bad I felt for her. I would never hurt any of my sisters.

Dad made it back before the school bus came and wanted to know what was wrong, but he didn't have to ask. He knew. The bus was coming down the mountain, and I could hear it coming across the bridge. The bus came to a stop with about ten students aboard, each of them looking out at me while he was giving me a major whopping with the end of a horsewhip. He was mad, and I was mortified. I was way too big to be whipped, and my friends on the bus were watching me get the whopping of my life. Mr. Andy Densmore was the bus driver. He was not happy with what my dad was doing to me and said something like, "Hurry up and get in here, Will!" Heck, I was trying, but he had a good grip on me.

When I finally made it on the bus, my pants were smoking. I was trying not to cry, because I thought I was too old to do that. Our dad would not let my little sister go to school that day and took her back to the house. As the bus was leaving, the kids started laughing at me. Conley did not want to sit with me, and Francis was furious with me. This was not a good day.

Within an hour after I got to the school building, everyone knew what had happened to me. Every once in a while, someone would say, "I smell smoke," and again they would laugh, but I deserved this whooping. I really did. Later on, I would have to come back home and face my mom and sister. I figured that was going to be the worst part, so I considered my options. I was way too young to run away from home, but I was thinking about it. What a heck of a thing for me to believe that I was a young man. I felt like a zero.

Lena Elizabeth was OK when I got home. I hugged her and tried the best way I knew how to let her know I hadn't meant to hurt her. Mom was a different story. She didn't say anything but just gave me that *look*. I was wondering if she was thinking about hitting me with a stick of stove wood, but she didn't. In a few days, it was over. I had learned a lesson the hard way, but sometimes that's the best way.

Conley and I were growing up, and in some ways, we were growing apart. I was involved—or at least wanted to be—in more school activities, like basketball, volleyball, and softball, pony-league baseball. This was not Conley's thing. I don't know if he ever liked sports. I think he felt that he wasn't very good, but he was, in my opinion. Later on, he was in a program that Mr. Ralph, our basketball coach, was teaching about how important exercise was. Mr. Ralph had picked Conley to be a part of this hour-long program and to participate in a push-up contest. This was held in the gym with all the school kids from elementary and high school sitting in the bleachers. My little brother was on the stage with another student doing the push-ups. Mr. Ralph was counting. They reached thirty, and at forty, both were still looking good. Then the other student was beginning to slow down, but not my little brother. He was at forty-eight, forty-nine, and fifty. That was all the other guy could do. Conley also stopped at fifty, but I knew he could have done more. He told me later that he stopped so that it would be a tie. I had a fit, because I wanted Conley to keep on going and show the whole school how strong he was. I wanted him to win. I thought about working him over, but then I really considered how strong he was and had second thoughts. I asked him why he stopped, and he said, "Fifty is a good number to stop at."

Later, I was selected to play on the junior basketball team and went with the seniors to play most of their games. We played first, and then, later in the evening, the seniors played. I was going to places like Austinville, Priceville, Arab, Cotaco, Hartselle, Molton, and Decatur. These were places that I had never been before or even heard of, except Decatur. For me, this was a great adventure. We rode with the coach or the principal and with some of the parents who had cars. It really was fun. I wanted to do all of this like the other students who didn't have as many chores at home as I did. The coach and other team members were counting on me to stay after school to practice, but my dad had different ideas. I had work to do at home, so it was almost impossible for me to stay after school. It was impressed upon me that I had to pull my load; if I didn't, someone else had to do my part. I knew that, yet down deep inside, I wanted to play some.

I had one more major whipping to get, and it was a bad one. I was growing up fast, but not too big for our dad to whip me. There was a game practice at my friend J.C.'s house not far from the Hulaco store. I got off the bus at his house with the idea to practice for a short while and then head home. The time got away from me when we played, and before I knew it, the sun was going down, and I had over three miles to walk home. I ran the whole three miles, and about a half-mile from home, I saw dad coming after me and he was not smiling, I knew what was in store for me, and there was no way that I could reason with him when he was mad—no way. I tried to explain, but he had his mind made up and I could tell that he was very upset with me. I wanted to keep on running, but I knew that wouldn't work, so why not get it over with?

He took longer than I expected, and he hurt me pretty bad with his big switch. When he let me go, I ran as fast as I could for the house. When mom saw me, she was beside herself. She had to doctor me up, using cream from the milk on my back and bottom. Even my arms and legs needed it. My mom—my buddy—stood up for me, here. She was mad when she saw the blood and how I looked. She was mad to the point of crying. I don't think I had ever seen her like this before. She went right to the front porch, where he was sitting and asked him how he would feel if she took the horse whip to him in that manner. I think that if she'd had a whip, she would have used it on him right there in front of me. She was right in his face, and her hands were going every which way. She would not put up with any of her children being treated that way. I was so upset with everything. I was thinking was I that bad of a kid? Did I really deserve a major whipping? What was I doing that was so wrong that I deserved that kind of punishment? I knew mom was on my side and that things would work out some way somehow.

He stayed clear of her for a week or so, not even speaking at the supper table. That was okay with me and, for sure, my mom. I could have cared less if he ever spoke to me again. Mom was on my side, along with my grandpa, who took me for a walk down through our pasture down to the creek that same evening. We sat on a log by the water, and I had a good cry, while he talked to me. I had scars for a long time. I think all my siblings felt sorry for me, but they couldn't show any concern while our dad was around.

I learned a very valuable lesson here: never dish out punishment when you are mad. As far as I am concerned, there is nothing wrong with correcting a child, but any kind of whipping is wrong in my book. There are so many other ways to get the point across.

That was the last whipping I ever got.

I was growing up to be a young man, and by now, I was thinking about what the future held for me. I knew the poor farm was not an option, and I was ready to leave anytime to get away from all of it. I had a few more years to go before I was out of there, and they were not going to get any easier.

Chapter 10

Hulaco, The Best General Store Ever

There on Rural Route One was the very best of all the country general stores. It was on Highway 67, about three miles from our house in the hollow. With a large garden and the rolling store that came by our house once a week, yet there was always something more we needed from the big general store. Usually, we made the trip on a Saturday afternoon.

Hulaco was where all the action was; the farmers and local people met there to relax, to socialize, to discuss all kinds of topics from farming to politics. Some gathered to play checkers, washers, to set on a nail keg or on an old wooden bench to play all kinds of card games. This was the place to be on a Saturday afternoon and more so if you were a young kid. Lots of the country folks went there to watch a new thing called "television." Everyone would gather around and watch cowboy shows, baseball games, or whatever was playing on the black and white television, and they were in awe at how this thing worked. Later, it would be in red, green, and blue color. A few years later, it was in real live color. That was a first for us, a television set was at the top of the list of all the wonders we had witnessed up until then. For me, it was an amazing thing to see. We could have spent the whole day there, but there was way too much work on the farm for us to lay around the store and do nothing, about a half hour was all the time we had to goof off.

At the Hulaco country store you could buy almost everything you ever needed for the farm and home, including work shoes, Sunday slippers, all kinds of clothing...even Sunday clothes. We called them store *boughten* clothes. There were tables of kitchenware, plates, tablecloths, and pots and pans. Another table had cloth, hats, caps, bonnets, hairnets, and so much more. For the farm, there was every kind of tool you would ever need, like axes, horse collars, trace chains, yokes, horseshoes, bridles, bits, plow shears, handles, hoes, pick sacks, rakes, and on and on. Then there were stacks of flour, fifty pounds and twenty-five-pound cotton sacks with all kinds of print, checks, stripes, and solid colors. Then on the other side were feed for livestock in fifty-pound cotton cloth sacks with so many different colors also.

The store had a porch with a roof that ran all across the front; there were two gas pumps up close to the porch; it was a busy place most of the time. The owners, Mr. Jake Walker and Mr. Hershel Latham, were the best people that you would ever want to meet. Both were good to everyone that came along. Things were reasonably priced and service came with a smile. They knew everyone for miles around. They often gave credit to those who needed it; there was no interest...people just paid back what they owed. It was the best place in the world for me to be on a Saturday afternoon.

Next to the store was a barbershop. Mr. Kermit Powell would give you a hair cut with his hand clippers, and it cost twenty-five cents. Later, he bought clippers that made a funny noise; they were electric. I liked the old hand clippers the best. The barbershop was a great place to sit and listen to all the men talk. It also smelled good.

Next to the general store was a very up-to-date gristmill. Here we hauled corn and hay that was mixed with cottonseed meal that was ground up as feed for our livestock. Also, the same corn was used to make corn meal. This was a larger mill than was at Ryan Crossroads and, again, it was a sight to see as everything was easily turned into feed and meal.

Next door to the gristmill was the wonder of wonders; a large cotton gin. As a kid, I was amazed to see how all this worked. The powerful whine of the motors as they went into action to make everything work was breathtaking. We would haul about 1,300 pounds of raw cotton in our steel-tired wagon and stop under a movable light suction spout. Then one of the workers inside would give you the signal for you to start. I would use that spout to suck all the raw cotton that we worked so hard to pick up and into the gin area. This would take only about fifteen minutes to complete. When that was finished, I would hurry around the back and tie up the team and go back inside and just watch how all that cotton became a five-hundred-pound bale. When it came out of the press, just one guy would roll it out onto a two-wheel cart that he had to be balanced so he could push it to the storage area, to be sold later. The whole process took only about thirty minutes. When all this was finished, the seed was sent to the gristmill to be ground. We used the ground cotton seed for protein to feed our livestock. Hauling the cotton to the gin was always a pleasant break for me, but when it was all done, I was on the way back to the cotton patch with my pick sack to start the process all over again. Since we were sharecroppers, we only got one bale out of three for our work. This was our way of life back then. It was a very poor way to get ahead in life, yet we were lucky to have Mr. Dewitt Crawford who was a very good landlord, a home, and food on our table. We could have had it a lot worse...or *worser* as we used to say. I only needed to count my blessing.

Chapter 11

Teenage Years

As most of us know, fitting in is something that we have to deal with as we grow up. If you don't fit in with the group, you're mostly out in left field by yourself. I turned thirteen years old in 1954. I was looking forward to the teenage years. By now, I was becoming aware of things that I had not noticed before. I was entering the real world, and becoming a teenager was the next step up the ladder. The clothes we wore, how we wore them, the way we looked, how we combed our hair or had it cut, the way we talked, and a hundred other things started to influence my way of thinking about myself, others, and my surroundings. I knew I was just an average kid. I knew I could get good grades if I applied myself, but I never thought I was any better than anyone else. In fact, I thought the opposite. For sure, I did not fit in with the in-group. Yes, even this small school with only fifteen students in my class had that group of people who thought that they were better and more popular than others.

Gosh, I really wanted to be liked just for who I was. I didn't want to be the top guy, just one of the guys. I think most of us feel that way. I wanted to be good at basketball, baseball/softball, and volleyball. We had no football at our small school. Far the most part, I was pretty good. Other students and coaches said I was good too. When I couldn't be at practice for some reason (and that was often), the coach would be upset with me, and some of the other students would say that they missed me not being there. That was a great thing to hear, and at this time of my life, I needed so much to hear that. I was a hustler and really gave each sport all that I had, and then some, just to prove that I could do it.

At six feet tall, I could jump and grab hold of the ten-foot-high basketball hoop. If the ball came even close to me, I was the one to get the rebound. My favorite sport was volleyball, and here I really excelled. Everyone knew I was one of the best, yet when the coach sometimes picked the captains and said, "Let's choose up and get started," there were times that I would be the last one selected. For me, that was the pits. Now I know that's just life, but back then, it was the worst feeling, especially for me. I know others probably handled it better and just let it pass.

With me as the oldest, this was not just a "me" thing. I wanted my brothers and sisters to be well dressed, to look good, and be well liked also. I wanted them to really try hard to give their very best and be good at what they did. Francis shared my thinking. As far back as I can remember she did everything that she could to look pretty...and she was. By then, she was eight years old and close to five feet tall. She was a redhead and was always fussing with her hair. It had to be cut just right—a job only I could do that pleased her. I think she knew then that I would cut her hair to make her look pretty....and she did. I was proud that she was my little sister.

I always thought that Conley was a great-looking guy...I still do. He was about five feet, six inches tall; always smiling and was easy to talk too. He had better looking teeth than I did, and his hair looked better than mine when it was combed back (I had that darned cowlick). He had a calm type of personality—easy going—and I have always liked that about him. Conley did not care all that much about sports, though. We went different ways on this.

By the end of 1955 I had another brother Thomas Randolph and two more sisters, Juanita and Rachel. All of us were born at home, except Juanita and Rachel (and later John). When Wanda was born, I remember our dad telling Conley and me to take the other children out to the barn or go for a walk. A black car would later drive into our yard, and a well-dressed man with a black bag would get out and go in the house. About an hour or so later, he would leave. Dad would call us back and there lying beside our mom was the cutest little girl you would ever see. She was so little—about five pounds. We all wanted to hold her. A little over a year later, Thomas was born. We had to leave the house again, and Conley said, "Oh no! Not another one." Thomas Randolph McCollum was the best-looking baby boy ever.

The family was growing at almost one new member a year. It was a good thing we now had that 4x8 sheet of plywood on the kitchen table. All of us had to pitch in while Mom took care of the babies. We helped with the feeding, holding, and yes...changing the diapers. For me, having a lot of children around was a good thing, but it meant even more work for my mom and the rest of us.

Being blessed with so many great looking brothers and sisters was for me something that was so very special. Even to this day they are great looking people. I am so proud to have been born their big brother. All my sisters are beautiful ladies, it makes me smile just thinking of them. The girls work just as hard as us boys. Everyone had to do their share....that was life.

As far as dad was concerned, our chores and farm work took precedence over school activities. At least that's how I perceived it. It was our living, and that was how we survived. If we did not work, we would not eat. Feeding all those kids took money, and to get money we had to work, so dad worked part-time here and there and was still the janitor at the school.

Conley and I worked when and where we could to make a few dollars, as well. By now, our dad would give Conley and me a few dollars to buy our own school clothes. It took more money than we had most of the time. For the most part, all the children couldn't participate in the activities at school if it cost any extra money. Therefore, I had to work double time just to have a pair of basketball shoes or those heavy white socks, and they had to be just the right kind, of course. I had to fit in with the other players, you see.

I don't mean to sound like I felt sorry for myself here. Well, maybe I did, but looking back, I was a blessed kid; life was good, I felt good, and I had great brothers and sisters. I was healthy too. Beans and cornbread is good for you, and as my grandpa would always say, "It sticks to your ribs."

I had some really good friends in school and still do to this day I keep in contact with a few of them. I would sometimes stay overnight with them; we had a great time. I would practice my storytelling that I had learned from my grandpa. One time, I stayed overnight with my friend, Dewey England, who was a very good student, a great guy, and a heck of a softball player. His brother, Glen, was just a year older than he was and a very good basketball player. We had tons of fun together. Their mom was a really wonderful lady and a great cook. She always fixed something special when I was there, so after a great suppertime meal; we were told it was bedtime. All three of us went and crawled into the bed. All three of us were in the same bed. That was the way it was back then. Glen wanted to hear my ghost story—the one about the chained slaves. Of course, from listening to my grandpa, I was getting it pretty much perfected by then. I could moan and groan and scream, as if I were one of the slaves. Glen got so scared that he begged me to stop. Dewey was sitting up with the quilt wrapped around him. Later, their mom came in with some very strong words telling us to be quiet and get to sleep. I know that she knew that it was me making all the weird sounds.

I was now fifteen-years-old and on the senior basketball team. When we went to different schools to play, we would stop at a local hamburger cafe and get something to eat after the game. There were times that I would have to stay in the car, because I had no money to buy anything. That was not a good feeling, because I could smell those burgers and fries cooking. I was starving to death, so I tried to have at least a dollar on me whenever we went to other places.

One time, we went to Arab for a basketball game. After the game was over and as we were leaving, everyone wanted to stop at a corner café. We all piled out of the cars and went in. Everyone was ordering, and I looked at the prices and figured out how much I could buy with a dollar. A plain hamburger was 95 cents, so I ordered. The waitress brought it with fries, and, for the life of me, I could not turn down those fries. I was hoping that they would not be on the bill, but they were. I put the saddest look on my face and told her that I only had a dollar. I thought she was going to call the cops on me. Luckily my coach, Mr. Ralph came to my rescue with a quarter, yet it was embarrassing, since she made a big deal out of it there in front of everybody.

I know back then you had to work hard for a dollar. I had to learn to do without at times, and as a kid that was hard. Our dad would say that I could not have things that my other brothers and sisters did not have. He was right, but I thought that I had worked hard for what I wanted to spend. It was only a dollar, and yet it was a lot of money for all of us.

When I was in the tenth grade, our dad decided that Conley and I could do the janitor's job at Ryan School. I don't think either of us liked the idea, but we had no choice. We had enough work to do at home already. We now had to get up at 4:00 in the morning to do a few chores at home, eat a couple of biscuits, and then walk to school. In the wintertime, it was much more work. Conley would do the elementary school: sweep the floors, empty the trash, clean the chalkboard, dust and sweep up the outdoor toilets. As it got cold, he would start fires in each of the rooms. Sometimes, it was not easy getting the fire going. There were five rooms, five stoves, five fires to start. He would then sweep the hallway and the coatrooms. All of this had to be finished in time; the rooms warm by 7:00 a.m. because school started at 8:00. He would have to make sure coal was in the bucket and all the ashes taken out before the 8:00 a.m. bell sounded. If he finished early, he would come and help me at the high school. I was trusted with the keys.

I would first unlock all the doors and let Conley get going. Then I would do almost the same jobs he had to do in the grade school. I had eight rooms to do, plus the gym, a long hallway, library, and a study hall room. There was a furnace that heated water for steam, and it was a bugger to get it going. I never perfected the art of starting a fire there. Sometimes, it would get going, and sometimes it took forever to get a hot fire started. That was the first thing I did, because it seemed to take longer to heat the high school. I would get started, and if the steam wasn't getting hot after an hour, I would have to go back down there and see what else I could do. I was frustrated with myself if the building was not getting warm by 7:00 a.m., because I wanted to do a good job.

Conley and I would help each other when we could. I would check on him to see if he needed help, and he would do the same for me. By the time we got all that finished, we both looked like we had worked in a coal mine. I would have Conley come over to the boys' restroom where there was running water so that we could get ourselves cleaned up as best as we could. I made it a point to make sure his face, hands, and clothes were as clean as possible, and he would check me out to be sure I was ready for the school day also.

At times, the other students would make nasty remarks about us being janitors. I took it much harder, since I hated that job. There were a number of times during a basketball game I would have to go get a mop and clean something up, while I was still wearing my basketball shirt and trunks. For me, this was embarrassing, because the other players were watching, and other students were sometimes snickering.

Mr. Ryan, the principal, was a great guy to work for, yet he wanted things done just right; he always checked to see that we were doing a good job. Conley and I would work hard at this. This was really a full-time job; we had to really hustle to get everything done.

The check at the end of the month was made out to our dad. It was in the amount of $81.00. On one hand, that was a lot of money back then, but on the other hand, it was a lot of work. Even then, it wasn't enough for all of us to eat in the lunchroom at noon. Conley and I decided to let our younger brother and sisters have a hot lunch, and he and I took either a loaf bread sandwich with a fried egg or sometimes sugar with butter in a biscuit. Sometimes we took both. We did all of this to survive as a family. Conley and I were part of all this yet; we did not like being janitors.

When we played basketball at home, there was a lot of work to do after the game. I had to give the gym floor a quick going over, clean the bleachers and the hallway, empty the trash, make sure all the lights were turned off, and the building locked up. Then I would have to walk home by myself and, most of the time, it would be close to 10:00 when I got there. I would be cold and tired and turn into bed and curl up around Conley to get warm. He would fuss and carry on. He definitely did not like me getting into the warm bed when I was that cold.

The lunchroom at school threw all the scraps and garbage away, so our dad asked if they would put all that in a five-gallon bucket and let me bring it home for the pigs, and they agreed. Before I got on the school bus, I would have to go get that bucket. Then I'd carry it to the bus and take it home for those lucky pigs. It always smelled good. I would usually check to see what was in the bucket. There were sometimes whole apples and oranges and other good food right on top. This was pretty good garbage. Those pigs were eating better than we were.

By now, I was figuring out my plans and checking into all the possibilities, for I knew this kind of life was not for me. I wanted to see what was over the next mountain. There just had to be something better for me out there. There were some things at home now that I had problems with. I had some wonderful brothers and sisters that were still just kids and still growing up. As most of us know, we have to do what we have to do. I think it is really neat when some folks live, work, and raise a family in the same area they have always lived, but I wanted to see the world. I wanted to climb the mountain and see the view from the top. I just had to see what was on the other side.

I was not going to ride this bus forever; somewhere, someplace the bus would stop and I would get off.

Chapter 12

DECISION TIME

For me life has always been exciting. With all the ups and downs, I knew I was living in the best of times. To survive, people need knowledge, a lot of common sense, an education, and need to be well read. I had these, *and* the ability to comprehend and understand the challenge that lay ahead of me, which is so important. The decisions we make early in life will set the directions we travel along life's pathways. Back in 1958, at the age of 16, I was weighing my choices and trying to think things out. Now, as I sit here, so many years later, I have two different emotions working inside me, both somewhat unsettling.

When you leave a place, there are always emotions and memories that linger in your mind, and many questions you ask yourself long after you're gone: Did I do the right thing, and what if? There are a lot of what-ifs. No one can make that choice for you; it is something you have to decide for yourself, and you usually don't know for sure if you have made the right decision, until later in life. Sometimes, one decision does not outweigh the other. In my case, it did. It was the right decision, then, and if I had to do it all over again, today, I would not change a thing.

One's attitude about life and about so many things in general is important, and for that reason, I decided in my teenage years I would be in charge of my attitude, be positive, hold my head up high, and be proud of who I was. This is all credited to a teacher and coach who were a great inspiration for me, and I think for others, as well.

Mr. Coy Putnam talked about attitude a lot. This teacher was as plain as an old shoe. He stood about five feet, five inches tall, and he was short-legged. At forty-five years old, he could outrun most of us in a good old-fashioned foot race. He had a way about him that projected success, and he did not allow anything to get in the way. I adopted one of his phrases: "Always try to be just a little better than excellent." I use that saying from time to time when someone asks me how I am doing. I say, "I am just a little bit better than excellent." They always give me that look and say, "Wow!" I've never forgotten Mr. Putnam and how upbeat he always was. This thing called *attitude* was going to play a very important part as my life unfolded, and it still does to this day.

I was so lucky to have such a great person as my basketball coach. Mr. Lester Ralph was my idol back then, a great person, teacher and one of the best basketball coaches ever. At over six feet six inches tall, he was my role model. He always encouraged all of us to be the very best at whatever we did. I was so fortunate to have wonderful teachers they really do make a different.

For such a small school we had one of the best basketball teams in Morgan County. The team was led by two great guys in my class. Hubert Thompson and J.C. Ralph; they were good people, great students and two of the best basketball players I believe in the state of Alabama at that time. It was an honor for me to be on the same team with them.

I was still doing pretty well in school I enjoyed learning things. I needed a little help from time to time and more study time to get good grades. For me, a B average was an attainable goal. There were a few subjects that I could get an A in, like history, science, typing, and of course, physical education.

If I did not get time to really dig into a subject, or if I had a hard time understanding it, then it was a C. I had a heck of a time understanding Algebra. It was interesting to me, but I completely failed the first mid-term test—a big, fat F. It just about brought me down—an F. I asked Mr. Ryan, the principal who was also the teacher, if I could retake the test. He said that was not the school's policy, but I had to pass this. I needed some extra help. Our dad was good at math, but by now, he and I were not seeing eye-to-eye on a lot of different things. I did ask him, but it had been twenty years since he had graduated from high school, and he acted like he didn't want to help anyway. My fellow student, Dewey, was getting very good grades, so I cornered him and made him an offer he could not refuse. Of course, he said yes, but time was a major problem. He had things to do, and I had things to do. He rode one bus, and I rode another. It was hard for us to find enough time to work together, but we did. I helped him with History, and he helped me with Algebra. On the next test, I had to pull a B or at least a C+ to get back in the race. If I didn't, I was going to fail the course. I had never failed a course before and wasn't about to start. On the next test, I got a plain C and then later, a C +. Mr. Ryan passed me, but it was with the slimmest margin.

As I was getting into my mid-teens, I—like so many other kids—thought I knew everything. Conley had been my buddy for so many years, but now he and I were drifting apart, mostly because of my dumb way of thinking. I was going—or at least trying to go—ninety miles an hour. Conley, on the other hand, was like a big ship on a slow and steady course. He would have made a great captain on a large ship. I was now a full-fledged type A, and he was a type B. We clashed. I knew for the most part just how far I could push him. We would have a few spats, but if I got too rough or to physical, he started giving me that "I am going to get even with you" look. One time, he and I were doing something, and he was not going at the speed I thought he should be going. I pushed or shoved him, and he almost fell. Then, in a slow, clear voice, he told me that if I ever did that again, he would make my head hurt. He said it in a way that I got the message. See how stupid I was, but also how fast I could learn a lesson with the right circumstances.

Sometimes, life gets in the way, and you have to stop and take a different path. Now a fork in the road was coming, and I had to decide what was best for me. I had read everything in our school library about careers. I would have loved to have the grades and the money to have gone to college at Auburn University, then on to flight school to become a pilot, but that wasn't going to happen. By now, I had pretty much decided that the military was my best option. I had read everything that the Marines had left at our school. I was leaning their way, mainly because I liked their uniforms. I liked the toughness and the challenge, but I definitely wanted to be more than just a foot soldier.

After a number of talks with the Army recruiter, it was obvious that the Army had so much more to offer me. I took the one hundred-question test and did very well. It was easy and only a preliminary test, but the recruiter informed me that the Army was looking for recruits that had a good general knowledge aptitude. I remember him asking me what I was good at, and without thinking, I told him I was good at picking cotton, running, basketball, and volleyball. Of course, the Army didn't have much use for those skills at that time, but he assured me that I would be given the opportunity to continue my education while serving. I was only sixteen years old and could not enlist until I was seventeen. Then my parents would have to sign. I was eager, and March was a few months away.

Mr. Ralph knew I was thinking about leaving school. He wanted to have a sit-down talk with me. He listened while I did a lot of talking, reasoning, and explaining. Most of it was personal. He was a good listener and helped me reason through things. He knew so much more than I thought about my situation, and he tried to put himself in my shoes. Mr. Ralph said the decision was mine, and we left as friends. We remained that way for many, many years.

Teachers almost always vote for staying in school and tell you to hang in there, dropping out is not the best way out. I was being pulled hard both ways. Being the oldest of our clan, I needed to set a precedent for my younger siblings to follow. Some of my fellow students, my coaches, and my teachers were not the least bit happy with me joining the military before I graduated. It was hard. I'm even trying to somehow justify it now as I write this. Was I a quitter looking for an easy way out? Was I being selfish and dodging my responsibilities? Was I letting someone else carry my load? I was too young to reason at the time, but today I agree that my teachers were right. I'd find myself saying the same things: "Stay in school. You can do it, and this will pass. A high school diploma is worth a lot." My teachers—most of them anyway—left a great impression on me. They were there to help, guide, push, challenge, and encourage me (and everyone else) in the right direction.

My mind was racing about whether or not I should join the military, so I used the old method of listing my options. I used a plain sheet of paper and drew a line down the middle. On one side I listed all the reasons for joining, and on the other side, I listed all the reasons against it. After a long look, I chose the Army, passed the physical and all the aptitude tests. I was ready for a change.

With reluctance, my parents signed, giving me permission to enlist. The date was set. The recruiter told me to start packing my bags, but heck, I had nothing to pack. I only had two pairs of jeans, two shirts, and some old shoes.

It was quiet at the supper table that evening. I felt like everyone was avoiding me, and no one was talking. For the last sixteen years, I had been present at that table during so many stories and so many wonderful times. We talked history, politics, news of the day, new babies, and a hundred other subjects at that table, but it was different that night. As the evening came to a close, Conley, Thomas Randolph, and I crawled into bed for the last time together. T R was crying and wanted to know if I was really leaving. I told him I'd be gone only for a while, as I tried to be truthful but gentle with saying the right words. I curled up around him while the tears came to my eyes. We talked and cried together, and I tried to tell him that the time would come later when he would also be leaving home. At this point and time in his life, he did not understand. We both cried ourselves to sleep. This was not how I thought it was going to be.

My dad was not talking, Mom did not look at me, and Conley was not saying much…he never did. Francis couldn't believe I was really leaving. Thomas Randolph was counting on me to be a big brother. Lena Elizabeth had that sad look about her, and Wanda just did not understand. Juanita was four years old and Rachel three. Dolan hadn't been born yet.

Mr. Putnam wanted me to stop by the school before I left, but I choose not to. It would have been more than I could have withstood. Sometimes, it is too easy for me to cry.

I left early that morning as the sun was coming up; I had to be in Decatur, which was forty miles away, by noon. I had to walk three miles to the country store at Ryan Crossroads; the recruiter was picking me up there. Then I had to catch a bus to Montgomery. Conley was doing the morning chores now by himself and that made me feel low. Lena Elizabeth, Francis, Wanda and Thomas Randolph were up and getting ready for school. My feelings were going every which way. Even now, it's hard to write this. Tears still fill my eyes.

I looked at Conley and said, "I will see you later, Buddy."

He just whispered, "Okay," and looked the other way.

There were no hugs, no "Be careful," no "Good luck," no "Good bye."

Chapter 13

Leaving Is Hard

Walking down the dusty gravel road away from Rural Route One, which had been my address for sixteen years, was both sad and exciting. I knew even then that what lay ahead most certainly outweighed what was behind me. From this point on, it was up to me—only me—to survive, to make it, to be somebody, to succeed at this thing called life. From this day on, I knew that I could not fail; I had put all my eggs in one basket. Today was the beginning of a journey that would last a lifetime. All the unknowns that lay ahead of me were things that I could not comprehend. It was a bit scary to say the least. I really wanted so much to be successful, and I also wanted my family to be proud of me, to understand and be there to cheer me on. I have always needed that acknowledgment, the words of affirmation, and the "Atta boy." I still do.

As I walked out of our yard there in The Hollow that spring morning, the day was just coming alive with a warm breeze. I just kept walking and did not want to look back. From now on, I only wanted to look forward. My baggage consisted of a toothbrush and some baking soda in a Prince Albert tobacco can, one short-sleeve shirt, and a pair of faded blue jeans in a paper sack. I had four dollars that I left under the pillow on our bed as a surprise for Conley and T. R. Out on the country dirt road and past the Y where we had waited for the school bus, I saw that old mailbox that had been hit with hundreds of rocks. I walked across the wooded one-lane bridge over the creek where we would swim and bathe in the summertime. I looked at the side of the hill where I saw last year's cotton stalks. Just a few months ago, I had pulled a seven-foot pick sack. I continued up the long, winding gravel road and around the curve to the top of the hill.

It was the first week in April of 1958; spring had arrived on Rural Route One. Trees were coming alive on both sides of the road. The smell of honeysuckles, pine trees, and wild flowers lined the banks of that dusty country road. I passed the old shed that reminded me of the ghost story of the chained-up slaves. I remembered walking the cow up and back on this road. Conley and I had walked it many times, before the sun came up, as we left to build fires and clean the school rooms. My mind was full of those memories.

The tears came easy. A part of me wanted to go back and hug all my brothers and sisters and tell them that I loved them. I really did love all of them. The word *love* was not spoken in our home very often, but I knew what it meant. Now, while walking away, I wanted to go back and say it out loud, so that they would know that I really did care about all of them, and so they would not forget me. I have always had the feeling that they would forget me. I don't know why. I wanted them to know that I was not leaving them for good and that I would come back to see them. I doubt they knew why I was leaving, why I wanted to live a better life, why I wanted off the farm. I wanted to go back and hold Juanita and Rachel. They were just babies. Would they remember that I was their big brother? I wished I could take them all with me to a better place to live. My mind was all messed up inside. I thought this would be easy. It wasn't.

Still, I kept on walking. I had made a promise, a commitment to the Army, and I felt that I must fulfill the contract. I had to start being a man and to keep my word. Somewhere, I always hoped I would start a new and better life, and now was my chance. Even today, I still remember all the things going on inside my head as I came nearer to the country store. It still makes me dizzy just like it did then.

As I came around the curve on that road, the morning sun was shining brightly. I was at a fast walk, hurrying not to be late. As I came out of the woods, I could see the Army car at the country store there at Ryan waiting for me. He asked if I was ready to go. I didn't have to think. I said "Yes," and we were driving away from where I had been raised, leaving behind my old self and all of the memories. On the way to town, we talked, and I told him I was scared but wanted to go. He assured me that I would be just fine and that he had a lot of faith in me. He told me that I would not be the only one going through all this; there would be others whom I would get to know. I was assured that this was my chance to live a dream, to see the world. The experience would be much more than I could ever imagine. He said that he was a living example of all that. All this encouragement helped me feel somewhat better, and then he reminded me that I would be given every opportunity to continue my education. That was very important to me.

At his office in Decatur, pictures were taken and we completed more paperwork. Then we headed to the bus station. This was the first time I got to ride a Greyhound bus. It was so much nicer than the old school bus. They were really first class. I got on board with just that paper sack holding my things. It was just me and that sack. Looking out the window of the Greyhound bus, I kept my eyes on the outside world, as we glided southbound along the highway. Everything from this point forward was new to me.

The South was coming alive. Spring was in the air, and trees were coming back to life, turning a pretty green. All this was new, because I hadn't been very far from home—no more than forty miles. The recruiter had given me a meal ticket to eat lunch at one of the bus stops along the way. This was a first for me, and I didn't know how it worked. If I ate too much, would I have to pay the extra? I had no money, so I asked the lady how much I could eat with this meal ticket. She looked at me funny, as if I had been the first person to ever ask her that question and said, "Hon, you can eat all you want!" I was in Heaven. From this point on for the rest of my life, I was living a dream.

The adventure and excitement was intoxicating, and as of today, I still have not had my fill.

There was more paperwork at Montgomery, along with a number of other recruits going through the same procedures. One clerk asked me what my address had been for the last five years, to which I had an easy answer. All my life, it had been Rural Route One. The hustle and bustle of everything swept me up: hurrying around, going to different buildings, talking to people, completing my first ever physical—and hoping it would be the last, as we all followed each other completely naked along the yellow line.

I had left my paper sack with my stuff in it back where we were staying. When I returned, I learned that someone there thought it was trash and threw it away. Now, I only had the clothes on my back. That night, I washed my shirt, pants, and socks in a sink, hoping they would be dry by morning. They weren't, of course, but they were clean.

We spent one more day at Montgomery, while even more young men showed up, and then we loaded a bus to Fort Chaffee, Arkansas. I was leaving Alabama for the first time and was excited. It was my personal history in the making.

We stopped at some military barracks in Mississippi to spend the night. Then we drove straight on to Fort Chaffee. It was good to be with others who had joined and those who were drafted. We had fun talking and wondering what was in store for us. It was fun for me, at least. There were times that I wondered if I would make it or not, as I looked at others who were so much older than I was, so much more mature and educated.

Fort Chaffee to me was a nice place. Of course, any place was a nice place to me. We were given more tests and issued all our military clothing. There were so many items: real soft towels, (this was the first time in my life that I had a real towel) underclothes, socks, and a duffle bag to carry it all in. I had never known in my whole lifetime anyone who had that many clothes. I was also given a brand new tooth brush and real tooth paste by a Red Cross lady. I really liked that it made my day.

Later, at the health clinic, I think we were given at least a hundred shots. Well, it seemed like that many. We were there about a week, and by the end of that week, I was in uniform with the OD Ike jacket, brown shoes, and brown combat boots. Just before we departed, we went back to the supply room and were issued a green dress uniform. They informed us that we had to dye our brown shoes black. We thought it was a bummer, but we were in the Army now.

While at Fort Chaffee, everything was easy going. No one was hollering at us, and it was kind of laid back. I thought, *this isn't bad at all. I think I am going to like this man's Army.* I had by now met a couple of young guys I liked. One was from Birmingham. The other was from Athens, and he said the county sheriff had given him a choice—either jail or the Army. We stayed together through basic training. I think we all would have been happy to stay in Arkansas, but that wasn't going to happen.

We were back on the bus again, which was three buses by now. We were on our way to Fort Hood, Texas, and I was really excited about that. I had read a number of cowboy books about Texas, and now I was going there. I remember reading about General Hood, one of General Lee's generals that served with the Confederate forces during the Civil War. Fort Hood was named after him. Now, I was on my way where the longhorns ran and cowboys rode the trails, only I was riding a charter bus. They give us sack lunches to eat along the way, and it was a great lunch and a wonderful ride. Going west, wearing the same type of uniform that so many heroes had worn before me, I was all smiles.

We arrived at Fort Hood late in the afternoon. I noticed how clean it was and how nice the grass was trimmed. Everything looked so nice. I wondered who they hired to keep it looking so darn good. The loudest Army sergeants in the world greeted us. What they were all so worked up about I didn't know. All of them were downright angry men. They were called drill sergeants. Little did I know that years later I would eventually become one of them.

This was nothing like Fort Chaffee, Arkansas. We had to run with all of our clothes in a duffel bag, which weighed about forty pounds, and then do push-ups with that bag on our backs. When we did not do them fast enough, we had to do them again…and again, and again. It took us forever to get to our barracks. The drill sergeants were hollering and giving orders, sometimes right in our faces. Gosh, what had I gotten myself into? I had never heard people talk like that before and hadn't read anything like this in the career information at my school's library. It seemed like we couldn't do anything right; we could not please any of them. I heard this one drill sergeant yelling at someone who was doing something really dumb. I couldn't believe he was hollering at me.

We had our hair cut at Fort Chaffee, and now it was back to the barbershop for a real GI haircut. The barber didn't even ask us how we wanted it cut. The guy next to me looked like he had been scalped. We were assigned to barracks in alphabetical order, so I ended up in the third platoon.

So much was happening so fast. There were interviews, details, getting settled in, and there were drill sergeants everywhere. Now I knew who kept all the grass cut and everything looking so good. I remembered Coach Putnam and all the things he had talked about, especially that word *attitude*. I would make good use of it here…and it would pay off big.

Chapter 14

Basic Training

Military training is serious business. The drill instructors made sure we understood how important it was, and they had their own way of making sure we got it. For us, it was real; this was the training that would get us somewhat prepared for combat. The little things counted, like getting it right the first time and never forgetting the main thing. I had read a lot about the military, but this was all so new to me. First, we had to learn the very basics: marching as a group. This was not as easy as one might think. For the first week or so, when the drill sergeant said, "Right face," low and behold, someone would turn left. It was funny, as long as it wasn't me turning the wrong way, because the drill sergeant always made an example of it. He would have that person do at least twenty extra push-ups while we all waited, and then the GI would have to carry a rock in his right hand for the rest of the day. We were becoming soldiers now—the lean mean green machine. By now, we were working together as a team. We had to get it right as a team, and we had to survive as a team. I liked that. I remembered my basketball coach saying the same thing.

One day, we'd be learning how to stand, lunge, and fight, using our M-I rifles with a bayonet fixed at the end of the barrel, prepared to take a life. The next day in the classroom, we'd be learning how to perform first aid to save a life. I remember one guy who thought some of the first aid training was funny, and he was not taking it very seriously. He was not paying attention and was horsing around. The DIs made an example out of him. They simulated a sucking chest wound with him, made fun of the situation, and then let him die a fake death. He was dead for the rest of the day, and a guard was stationed over him to make a point. He had no chow, no water, and couldn't smoke, or do anything except lay on his back with a cover over him. He wasn't allowed to move and had to lie in one position the rest of the day. They had made a point, and he definitely got it. Letting a buddy die was not an option; we were being trained to do everything in our power to help our fellow soldier. We were becoming a band of brothers…we had to know that we could count on each other. The training was real...very real. This was serious—learning how to kill, then fighting to live another day, and doing everything possible to save someone's life. We had to work as a team, fight as a team, and survive as a team.

Each day was exciting for me. Most of us were getting the hang of things, or—I should say—getting used to the Army's way of doing things. Training for war was a dangerous and unthinkable thing for me, yet that is what I had signed up for. I wanted to be a good soldier, wanted to be the best at whatever the task was. Hand-to-hand combat was exciting, until it all soaked in. The drill sergeants made it very real. This was serious business, and part of me was scared to death, even while in training. The idea of "kill or be killed" was completely foreign to me.

We got paid once a month in cash; my base pay was $61 per month. Payday of course was a special day. We all had to line up alphabetically, and the drill sergeants would ask us questions, as we moved up one-by-one to receive our pay. We had to salute, give our names, rank, and serial numbers. Everything had to be just right, or they would make an example out of us in front of everyone. One sergeant would ask a first-aid question: "How do you stop bleeding?" Later, another sergeant would ask something else.

I remember one of the sergeants asking me what state was I from. I said, "Alabama, Sir."

He asked, "Who is your governor?"

I said, "Big Jim Folsom, Sir."

He smiled and said, "That's a good name for a governor." He then asked me what my permanent address was.

I said, "Rural Route One, Sir."

"Alabama?" He asked.

I said, "Yes, Sir."

I went forward, saluted, gave my name, rank, and serial number, and received my pay. After all the taxes and a saving bond were taken out, I received $38 in cash. I was a rich man. That is the first time in my life that I had had that much money in my pockets. Also, I now had started a saving plan with U.S. Saving bonds; I was going to become a rich man. I sent $20 home to my parents to help them out.

I had made friends with a fellow from Tennessee by the name of Curtis Daniel Mann. He was in my squad; he slept in the next bunk to me in the barracks. He lived as far back in the sticks as I did. He was a real hillbilly and therefore a fun guy to be around. He did not like his first name, Curtis; he wanted to be called Dan. We called him, "Dan the Man." When he said something smart to me, I'd reply with, "Yes, Private Curtis." Then he would give me that I-am-going-to-get-even-with-you look. He was slow in speech and slow in all his movements—never in a hurry. He and Conley would have been a good match.

We were now in the fifth week of basic training, and our platoon was doing well. This was the first time that we were given a pass to go to town if we wanted one, but we had to be back in the barracks for bed check by 10:00 p.m. Dan the Man had asked me one time if I knew what a whorehouse looked like. I said, "What? Heck no." He said he had always wanted to see what all went on there. He wanted me to go with him to Dallas, the capitol of Texas, just to look if there was one there. I remembered Billy Wayne, one of our neighbors back in Alabama who had just returned from serving a few years in the Army, saying that there were a lot of whorehouses in Texas. I told Dan that I thought the capitol of Texas was Austin. He said no, it was always the largest city in the state. I wondered if I'd learned that wrong. Dallas was too far away for us to go, anyway, but I decided to go with him if he went to Austin. He said, "OK. That's where we'll go."

We always had a barracks inspection every Saturday morning. Our barracks passed, and by around 10:30, Dan and I were wearing our dress khaki uniforms for the first time. We looked just about as new as any new recruit had ever looked. We both thought we looked pretty good with our spit-shined low quarters and a very close GI haircut. After checking each other out, we headed to the orderly room (company headquarters) to sign out. We had to stand in line, since there was a large number of other GIs signing out and going on pass, as well. As we approached the area, a drill sergeant was there checking each person and asking questions. He inspected us; looking us over to be sure we had our brass on right, our belt buckle and shoes shined, and a good haircut. Then he asked us a number of questions.

"Where are you going?"

"Austin, Sir."

"What are you going to do there?"

"Just look around, Sir."

"What are you looking for?"

"A whorehouse, Sir," Dan said slowly.

The sergeant started laughing, as did everyone else within the room. Everyone was looking at us and laughing. I thought, *what did he say that was so darn funny?* I don't remember what else was said, but we got the heck out of there because everyone was having way too much fun at our expense.

We waited outside our barracks to catch a bus to the small town of Killeen, which was only a few miles from Fort Hood. We were among a number who were going to town for the first time, after so many weeks being housed in the barracks. We felt like a herd of cattle that had been let out after being penned up for a while. Everyone was a buck private in his uniform with a GI haircut, on his way to town. We were quite a sight.

At the Killeen bus station, we purchased a round-trip ticket to Austin. We had to be absolutely sure that we returned in time and got back to our barracks before 10:00 p.m. If we missed bed check, we would be AWOL and in a lot of trouble. Gosh, this was something else, since we were now on a fancy bus heading to the capital of the great state of Texas. I was excited. We left Killeen at around 1:00 p.m., and the ticket said we would have to leave Austin at 7:00 p.m. That would get us back in plenty of time to make bed check. This meant that we had about five hours for a look-see there in Austin.

Dan was talking and acting like this was just a normal thing. He was so cool, and I just knew we would have great time in the big city. Dan was eighteen years old, and I had just turned seventeen. I was with someone who knew his way around, and for sure I would learn a lot from this old boy from Tennessee...at least that's what I thought.

I was getting hungry and couldn't wait until we got to Austin so we could get a hamburger and fries. It seemed like it took forever to get there. As the bus came into Austin, we both were looking out the window to see if we would pass anything that looked like a whorehouse or a sign that indicated one. We were disappointed. As we pulled into the station and exited the bus, we were all eyes, and I left it up to Dan to see which way we would start walking.

By now, I was starving, because we hadn't had lunch yet. For some reason, Dan was not hungry, and I was surprised, because he loved Army chow. We walked by a number of cafés, and my stomach growled each time we passed one. An hour later, we were still walking. It was close to 4:00 p.m., and I was dying of starvation. We walked down one block and back up the other side. I asked Dan if he knew for sure whether we had seen one or not. Would he know what it was when we saw it? He said we would know. "I'm sure that there would be a lot of good looking women there and that the place would smell good." The only thing I could smell was the hamburgers cooking as we passed by a restaurant.

Here we were, two buck privates with our Army uniforms on, walking and looking at every business along the streets there in Austin, Texas, a thousand miles away from home. This was a really big city. I wonder what those people thought as they watched us hoofing along the hot and dusty streets of the capital city of Texas. By now, I was wondering what my sisters would think if they knew that their big brother was out in a strange town looking for a whorehouse. I tried not to let my mind go there. I think we both thought that we would see a house or business with the word "Whorehouse" in blinking red letters. I asked Dan if maybe we should ask someone for directions. Maybe the telephone book would have a listing of them, but he said, "No, we don't want people to think we're not all that smart," so we just kept on walking and looking. I saw a cop car go by and thought about flagging it down; for sure, the cops would know where one was.

It seemed like we walked all over Austin. I was tired and wishing that I was back at Fort Hood, since it was about chow time. Food was the only thing on my mind now. I had forgotten what we came to Austin for. I was thinking about food and nothing else. Dan wanted to walk down a few more streets, but I said, "There is no way, Curtis. Why don't you just ask someone?" This was the second or third time I had wanted him to stop someone and ask. I reminded him, "We have to be back to the bus station before 7:00, you know," and by now, I didn't know if we even knew how to get back. Dan the Man was not what I thought he was. He didn't know any more than I did, which was nothing...zip. The only thing we saw that even came close to a blinking red sign was a building that said "Pancake House."

We walked back in the direction we had come from, and I made Dan go inside a little café to eat. After we sat down, he informed me that he had no money, and he wanted to know if he could borrow five dollars from me. I said, "What?! Curtis, you are dumber than a rock, you came all the way out here with no money?"

He said, "Private Mac, you call me 'Curtis' one more time, and I will rearrange your front teeth."

Yeah right, I thought. I was in control now; he was broke and trying to give me a hard time. I only had nine dollars myself.

By the time we got back to Fort Hood, I had two dollars left, since I had to buy Dan's supper. I was mad at him, he was mad at me, and now we had to go back and face all those ugly GIs who wanted to know how we came out at the whorehouses. I wished a hundred times that I had just stayed there in the barracks. I think they laughed at us for the next four weeks. They were having fun with us. I blamed it on Dan, and when he could, he blamed it on me. We laughed at all this for years to come. He still thought that Dallas should be the capital…I just smiled at him.

Looking back, I don't know what we would have done if we had found a house of ill repute. We would have just stood out on the street and looked, I guess. We only had nine dollars between us. I was definitely the dumbest kid who ever had walked the streets of Austin… or any street as far as that goes. Things worked out for the best; they always do, I think. Dolly Parton once starred in a movie with the title of *The Best Little Whorehouse in Texas*, and I have yet to see it. It's supposed to be funny, but it couldn't be any funnier than two kids walking the streets of Austin trying to find one. I have lived and witnessed so much in my life, but I have yet to see a building with blinking red letters that says, "Whorehouse."

In training, we were learning all about the famous M-1 rifle. It was always considered a weapon, never a gun. If someone called it a gun, the drill sergeant would have us doing push-ups until we fell on our faces. We had to disassemble it, clean it, and put it back together. We even had to learn how to do it blind-folded. We would be in the barracks getting ready for bed, and then a drill sergeant would come in and have us get our weapons. Then he would turn out all the lights and have us tear it down and then reassemble it there in the dark. This M-1 was a great weapon, and it was easy to take care of. However, the firing range was a place I did not like, because I was also afraid of this weapon. It kicked hard when it fired, and the shells would fly up and hit me in the face. If you weren't careful when you reloaded, it would smash your thumb. We called that an M-1 thumb. It really hurt. Back then, the targets were put out at 100, 300, and 500 yards away. If you missed the whole target, they would wave a red flag, which was called "Maggie's Drawers." I ended up missing the whole target a number of times and could not believe it.

That rifle hurt me when I fired it. I was afraid of this thing, and I never did like guns. The drill instructor asked, "How come a country boy like you cannot hit the side of a barn? If a hundred enemy soldiers were charging you, you would miss the whole bunch. You would not get even one. No wonder you couldn't find a whorehouse! You must be blind! You wouldn't even know what Maggie's Drawers looked like if they hit you in the face." I thought that was a low blow...and how did he know about the whorehouse deal?

So much has been written about basic training; so many stories have been told. For me, it was a great experience, a lot of work, some fun, and I made some great friends. I had learned a lot and loved almost all of it, but I was glad it was over. The minimum score to qualify on the rifle range was 160. My score was 161, the lowest score of all. The rest of my scores were good. I was becoming a soldier, and I was proud of it.

Graduation day was something else. There were so many people there to watch us march past the reviewing stand. Everyone cheered us on. Many parents, girlfriends, and other family members were there. It was fun meeting some of them after the parade was over. I wished that my family— my brothers and sisters—could have been there to watch me march by in my dress uniform.

We made it. We had been through a lot, and we knew we could accomplish so much more, if we worked as a team. I remained friends with a number of the people in my platoon for a long time. Dan the Man went into tank training, and I went into transportation training. We kept in touch for a long time. Later, he was killed in Vietnam. I wish he were here today. We would still be giving each other a hard time. He was a great guy. I really do miss him.

Private William McCollum

Chapter 15

Lower Than Whale Doo-Doo

Basic training was over, but the hustle and bustle of hurrying up just to wait had not ended. It was organized chaos, as all of us were getting ready to leave, either for home or move to another company area at Fort Hood, Texas, for more training. So much had been presented to us so fast, and now we had to move out. There was no time for sitting around. The Army did not babysit anyone. We all had to move out of the barracks, since new recruits would be arriving in a few days. Many were going on leave; others were staying there for a few days, waiting for orders to go to a different post. Still others were going to their Advance Individual Training (A.I.T.).

I wanted to get away from all that for a while but did not have the money to travel all that distance back to Alabama, since I had been sending most of my money home. I would have liked to have gone back and shown off my uniform, and I wanted to see my brothers and sisters. My sisters were just little girls, and it looked like I would miss seeing them grow up. In fact, I would miss seeing all of them grow up. It was mid-June in Texas, and it was getting hot. The next phase of my training did not start for three more weeks. If I stayed there, I was told that I would be put on all kinds' details: mowing grass, KP (kitchen police), guard duty, and a number of other duties. My drill sergeant encouraged me to take the two weeks leave. I had to find the money to go home or stay there and do all those dirty jobs. Dan the Man's family sent him a round trip Greyhound ticket to come home, but there was just no way I could find the money for a round trip ticket on a bus to go home. Even if I had the money, once I got to Decatur, there would be no transportation for me to use. My family lived forty miles from town, and they had no vehicles. It was best all the way around for me to stay there at Fort Hood.

The next day, I was told to have my bags packed and that I was moving down the street. A Private First Class (PFC) drove up to the barracks with a jeep, helped me load all my stuff, and drove me to the next training area, which was on the other side of Fort Hood. I would be staying there for the rest of my training. For the first week, I was the only one there in that big old barracks. It was lonesome, and I was feeling sorry for myself. Being the only one in the barracks was a hollow feeling. The building cracked and made all kinds of sounds, and it did not smell like it did when it was full of other GIs. It was my job to keep it clean, dusted, and all the floors waxed and buffed. Later, two more GIs came, and for the next two weeks (which seemed like two months), we cut grass, picked up trash, and worked in the mess hall. I washed trays and all the cooking utensils, peeled potatoes, and cleaned the mess hall from early morning to late evening. It was a long two weeks.

At the end of those weeks, others were returning from their leave. The barracks filled up, and we were ready for our advanced training. I was ready to get off all those details. Everyone talked about how much fun they'd had on leave and about seeing their families, wives, and girlfriends. For a while, I felt left out, but then I realized I had it made. I was lucky to be a soldier in the United States Army. I was proud to be there. I ate good, had clean sheets, had a place to stay, with good clean clothes to wear, clean towels, and everything I could have ever needed. I was the most fortunate fellow in the world; life was good.

We were still living in the old WWII barracks—twenty-two soldiers living downstairs and twenty-two living upstairs. We had the same setup with the latrine—ten guys using the latrine, showers, and bathroom area at the same time just like during basic training. We still had to wait in line to use the latrine. The stools were all in the same small room, five on one side and five on the other side, very close together. By now I was used to eight GIs taking a shower at the same time. This was community living at its best.

The barracks were all painted light sandy beige inside and out. The inside was not finished. It was just a plain building with six windows on each side and doors on each end. There were fire escapes at each end on the top floor. It was actually very accommodating, and this was home with all the necessities we needed. The floor was covered with brownish linoleum. We would wax it and then use a large hand buffer, and it would really shine. It was hot—really hot—there in Texas during July and August. Most days it would reach a hundred degrees or more. I was used to hot weather, but with twenty-two guys on one floor there in the barracks, you can imagine. The bunk beds were stacked two high, so the area was just one big room where we all slept side by side. There were two big floor fans, one at each end of the barracks, and that was our air conditioning. They blew at full speed day and night. Taking a number of showers was a must each day, just so we could get cooled off. We still only had a very small wall locker and a footlocker where we kept all our uniforms and other articles. All this was very efficient, and it worked out for all of us very well. The smell inside the room was wonderful, consisting of shoe polish, brass polish, clothing, blankets, which had that special kind of odor that I liked. This was the life back then, and, for me, it was really great.

We were getting the very basic of training for the first week. We were awakened at 5:00 a.m., and all forty-four GIs had to get shaved, cleaned up, make beds, and be ready for morning formations outside for reveille. Then we were off to the mess hall for chow and then back to the barracks to make sure everything was ready for a walk-through inspection. After that, we were back outside for an in-rank inspection and then off to training. The sergeants reminded us that we were still privates; "Private E. Nothing" they said, "The lowest rank in the Army." From time to time, they would remind us that we were lower than "whale doo-doo." (Here I am using kinder words.) We had moved down the street, but had not moved up in status in this man's Army. *Lower than whale doo-doo.* Gosh, even now that I was out of basic training, I was still a nobody.

While going through all my initial testing, I scored the highest in Law Enforcement and Transportation. At six-foot-one and one hundred, forty pounds, I was informed that I was too small and too young to be a military policeman, so it was decided that I would be trained as a heavy-duty truck driver. I often wondered what they were thinking—too small to be an MP, but large enough to drive those great big five-ton trucks?

My family never owned a motor vehicle or a farm tractor while I was growing up. The only time I had an opportunity to drive was while visiting one of our neighbors, first driving an old F-12 Farmall tractor and later, a 40 John Deere with a hand clutch. I fell in love with driving at a very young age and still love to be behind the wheel, heading down the road today. Therefore, when I was informed that I would be sent to Drivers' Transportation School, I was in hog heaven.

During the first week, we were in the classroom learning all about drivers' safety, the rules of the road. The word "accident" was said with a slam of a book to the floor. The book slam on the floor was to keep us awake in the classroom. Most of the time, it was so hot that we moved outside for the classes. It was also meant to bring home the point, "No Accidents. Ever!" Soldiers driving Army vehicles do not have accidents—SLAM! Safety was the name of the game; accidents were not tolerated in this man's Army—SLAM! We were taught that if we had a—SLAM—accident that we might as well bend over, stick our heads between our legs, and then kiss our rear ends goodbye. (Still using kind words…)

I was so glad to get out of the classroom and to the Motor Pool. There was row after row of Army vehicles. The little jeeps, three-quarter-ton trucks (like a pickup truck), two and a-half-ton trucks, the big five-ton with duel wheels, and semi-trucks, all painted with the Army olive green paint. I could not wait to drive all of them, but we still had a way to go before we got in the driver's seat and behind the wheel. It was a slow, yet tedious, process, because this was serious business. The instructors never let us forget the importance of this profession and, of course, the importance of safety. We would later be transporting troops, food, all kinds of fuel, highly explosive ammunition, and other dangerous materials. I never took any of my training lightly; this was a very serious assignment I was taking on. I wanted to be the best at this, since there was no room for the smallest of mistakes. At the age of seventeen, I was the youngest of all the others there undergoing this kind of training, so I was nicknamed "The Kid." I was not particularly fond of being singled out, so I decided that I would use that to show them I would be one of the best of the best.

As the training continued, I met some really great guys from all parts of the country. One guy named Mitchell was from Chicago. He was a really funny kind of person. He was my first Black friend, a real city fellow from the "Windy City," and I was a real country boy. We were a good but unusual match. He was twenty-three years old with a wife and one child back in the land of Lincoln. Mitchell had been drafted and was not in love with the Army at all. He also sent most all his money home and was a devoted husband and father. I liked that about him. He had been around the block in life and had a great job. When the draft called him, he had tried every way to get out of it. Now, he was just going to keep his nose clean, serve his time, then go back home to his family. He loved cars, but did not know how to drive a stick-shift vehicle, which is the only thing the Army had. The vehicles we were to be tested in were all of the combat type. Mitchell and I were a team during most of our training there and became one of my best friends.

All the vehicles had canvas tops. I loved that smell when I was inside the cab. By sheer statistics, out of the forty-something guys, some were just bound not to be coordinated enough, and driving a stick shift was a problem for them. At first, the driving was just there in a controlled area at the motor pool. It was fun watching, as some almost ran into each other. We all got that down pretty well, so we moved to the Fort Hood driving range to do some road driving. They tried to match up the driver with a co-driver who had some experience. It was again fun to see them trying to help each other, and there were a couple of near misses. I thought that this was going to be easy, as I watched others trying to get the hang of clutching and shifting.

The weather there was hot, not much rain, dusty, and windy, but it was my kind of summer. I was outside doing something that I really loved. We had one more phase of instruction to complete, which was out in the woods and was called "The Combat Course." Here we would ford creeks, and climb hills, which seemed to go straight up. We had to learn to shift while climbing a hill and practice stopping halfway up and start again. This was scary. One vehicle flipped over, when the driver lost control. The driver and the co-driver were hurt and sent to a hospital. The course was really rough; crossing a creek that was almost waist deep, backing up and hooking onto another vehicle on the side of a steep hill were dangerous tasks. There were more accidents and a lot of near misses. Then we had to learn how to drive at night, with only the minimum lights called "Cat Eyes." We could only see the lights at about twenty-five to thirty feet away. A couple of drivers made the wrong turn and ended up lost, but it was so much fun for me. I was driving all kinds of vehicles, and it was a piece of cake.

We were near the end of our training and were told that some of us would be going to Germany and that we would be assigned to the Third Armored Division near Frankfurt. We were then sent back to the classroom to learn all about German road signs and more safety. By now, there was no slamming a book when the word "accident" was said. We had had our share of them while training. There is so much to be said about how the Army does things; I always and still do think it works out pretty darn good. I learned a lot there, but I wasn't so sure I would be able to drive all over Germany without getting lost and ending up in another foreign country.

There was a truck rodeo during the last week of training. They had a course set up which we had to complete within a set time. "The kid from Alabama" finished first with the least mistakes and was promoted from Pvt. E-1 to Pvt. E-2 right there on the spot. I was in my glory and, again, now I thought I was somebody.

Later, one of the instructors came up and congratulated me…but informed me that I was still lower than whale doo-doo. Oh well.

Chapter 16

Shipping Out

After completing Basic Training and Advanced Individual Training, I was now settling into the Army way of doing things. I was very comfortable with myself, and at this early stage, I thought that this would be my career. It was exciting, it was new, and it was my thing. Of course, I was still seventeen years old and a high school dropout… what did I know?

When this phase of training was over, we were ready to be shipped out to our new home to perform the jobs for which we had trained. There were about forty-four of us who had completed the combat driver's training course. We had a few days of out-processing, and then we had to get our stuff packed to be shipped out…not that different from a cattle drive. Oh well. We were in Texas, after all. For me, every day was exciting—going to different buildings, doing paper work, more shots, attending briefings, and getting through a lot of "hurry up and wait." I was in my glory. I was very well taken care of and had more than I had ever had in my short life. I knew what was expected of me and was developing a soldier's mindset. Again, there is the right way, the wrong way, and the Army way. I knew when to talk and when to keep my mouth shut—a valuable lesson for everyone to learn, I think.

I knew that I was going overseas and could not comprehend all the travel and excitement that was still to come. A few of the guys were sent to other units at Fort Hood. Some were sent to Forts in Georgia and Kentucky. I was one of the chosen ones to be going to Germany, a place I had only read about in history books. We were told to have our things packed and ready to move out; the sergeants were always telling us that: "Get your bags packed and be ready to go."

Nobody had the roll-around luggage that you see at the airports today. We each had a large Army Green canvas duffel bag in which we packed all of our belongings. When the duffel bag was full, it weighed about forty pounds, but it seemed like a hundred pounds. It had a strap and a handle. Our names and serial numbers were stenciled on them. I still have mine today. We could also carry a small handbag with us. We called it an AWOL bag. The duffel bags were carried over the shoulder. It was a sight to see, as hundreds of GIs all lined up, each struggling to balance their load.

We had to be ready to leave at 04:00 ., which meant that we had to get up at 02:30 so that we could have everything inspected, cleaned up, inspected again, and then stand in front of our barracks to receive information. The buses were all lined up outside our company area, and I was all smiles as we were just about ready to leave Fort Hood, Texas, which had been my home for the past five months. We all got our bags loaded and boarded the bus. By this time, there were eight buses all lined up and ready to depart. It looked like all of Fort Hood would be shipping out. We were informed that we would be boarding a train at Austin, Texas, and would ride across the country to New York City. I was wide-eyed and in awe of being on a train. I do not think that I had ever seen a train up close. As we were departing the bus in Austin, the train was coming into the station. It was a sight to see how this humongous engine pulled all those cars. It came up very slowly and screeched to a stop. It was hard for me to contain my emotions. To this day, I am still intrigued with trains.

Now, riding a big iron horse, living, eating, sleeping, and just relaxing in those Pullman units was living like a rich man, to me. It was almost more than I could stand. I, a former barefooted cotton picker, was riding first class across the U.S.A. in a classy train car.

After we boarded, lunch was served, and it was even better than Army chow. Mitchell and I sat together and shared the same booth. He wanted the top bed, and I was okay with the bottom. It was over an eighteen hundred-mile train ride, and it took us about three days to get to New York. Along the way, the train would stop, and we could get off and look around for a few minutes. It was all GIs, and all of us were privates. It was quite a sight. We talked, laughed, and just had a great time. The service aboard the trains was first class, and the sleeping compartments were about as nice as one could imagine. There were porters who waited on us, which was a first for me. The food was the very best. Why couldn't we ride that train all the way to Germany?

We arrived around noon on the third day at the port of entry and, there, I saw the largest boat I had ever seen. Later, I was told never to call a Navy ship a boat. An officer outside the bus yelled for us to grab our bags and get into formation. Here, we had to line up in alphabetical order. We were called off by name, and then we hoisted our duffel bags onto our shoulders, grabbed the handbags, and walked up the gang plank to board this giant Navy ship that was to take us to the other side of the world. The excitement just kept coming my way.

I think, normally, when you board a Navy ship, you have to salute the flag officer of the day, as you come aboard, but we were so loaded down with our baggage, we didn't have to stop to perform this duty as we came aboard. Then we headed down into the belly of this giant floating vessel. This was completely new, since I had never heard, seen, or read about life on a troop ship. Believe me, it was a surprisingly new adventure for me. First of all, it was very crowded; there were hundreds of troops on board. The bunk beds were made of canvas and were five high with just enough room to sleep and that was it. You couldn't sit up or even rise up very much. The Navy made use of every inch of the ship. There were steam pipes, water pipes, and electrical lines, right above our heads that clanged and banged day and night. The rows of bunks were just wide enough between that you could hardly walk. We were stacked in like cattle on a boxcar. This was only the first few hours. It was going to get much worse, or as we used to say down on the farm…"worser."

When you live with that many guys in such a small space, you can only imagine how all this was going to smell as the days and weeks went along. There was a lot going on all at once, it seemed. First, we had a briefing on what to do in case of a fire, then what to do if we had to abandon ship, how to release the lifeboats, who went where and what was expected of each of us in case of an emergency. We did all this and even a dry run, before we had time to go to the bathroom, which the Navy called a "head."

I wanted to be on the top deck when we departed. The ship slowly began to move with the help of tugboats. There, Lady Liberty was standing with her right hand held high, as we slowly left the harbor. I wanted to see New York as the big ship slowly made its way to the mouth of the Atlantic but that was not to be, as I was selected for a storage-room detail right away. I was sent to the third level down to help sort and stack all the hundreds of duffel bags in alphabetical order. It was so darn hot and stuffy with all those full duffel bags. We were supposed to be relieved for chow, but it was after 2100 hours, when I found my way back to my sleeping area. I had missed the evening meal, so I went back up on the top deck. By now, the lights of New York City were far off in the distance. The ship was already out in the Atlantic Ocean. We had shipped out, and I had missed the whole show.

Life on a big Navy troop ship was something else. First of all, I am not—nor have I ever been—a seafaring person. Next, if I thought that forty-four men in one barracks was a lot, then hundreds of stinking, ugly GIs in the same size area out in the middle of an ocean was going to be a rude awakening (and more than half of them seasick). The ship rocked and rolled; the waves beat against the sides, and there were always a number of sick people lined up along the side rail heaving their guts out over the side. It was a sad sight to see. Remember, the bunks were stacked five high. That was not so bad, except when the top guy got sick and emptied his guts out on the four sleeping below. What an experience. Most of us were kept busy with some kind of detail each day: chipping paint, cleaning, mopping up the things other people had eaten and could not keep down. It was always some form of cleaning. Some worked in the mess area, and some were on guard duty or fire alert watch. Remember me saying that anything was better than picking cotton? Well, this was close. I hoped that, after a few days, I would get used to all this, but that never happened.

I was and have always been a good eater and have always like good food, but not when I was at sea. Nothing smelled good, and when I tried to eat, I had to hold on to my plate with one hand and eat with the other. Again, there was always someone who had to upchuck, while eating there in the mess area. I never got used to that. Who could? When using the bathroom or the "head," there were not just six stools facing each other. There were fourteen. Yes, twenty-eight stools in a small area. It was something else when you would see one guy sitting on the throne and another losing every morsel he had eaten right across from you. It was all you could do to look at his rear and hope that he did not go at both ends. Everything was very close together. I saw so many of our brave young men thinking they were about to die, right there in the bottom of that beast. Thus, I will say no more. Let me just end with this: the "Love Boat" has never interested me in the least.

I did not get very sick, but my stomach never quit churning, until both feet were safely planted on the European continent. It was a new kind of heaven for me. Being in a foreign country was like walking down history lane. Heck, even a ride to Tennessee was a foreign place to me, so you can imagine what this was like. We had to leave the ship in our dress uniforms, find our duffel bags, and get lined up and departed in an orderly fashion. I was never so glad to leave the Navy life behind and never look back. We docked at the port in Germany called Bremerhaven. I could just feel that everything was so much different: the trucks were different, and people were dressed differently.

I was all eyes, as I departed the big gray ship, and we all were glad that part was over.

It late September 1958; it was cool as we traveled across Germany on an old passenger train. It was clean and the food was great. The train traveled much slower than the American trains and was not fancy at all, but very practical. I believe we only spent about eight hours riding the German train. I was wide-eyed, as we rolled along the countryside through small villages along the way. I wanted to see everything. The train stopped at a large train station (the "Bonhoff"), in Frankfurt. There, a sergeant ordered me and seven others into the back of a five-ton, rough-riding combat Army truck, the same type that I would be driving later on. The drive took us through Frankfurt and out to the edge of town, where we would be living. It was a bumpy ride; the streets were paved with bricks or cobblestones. However, I was excited because I knew that, shortly, I would be at my new home. As the truck stopped, the eight of us were ordered to get out, get our bags, and follow the sergeant.

Chapter 17

Living A Dream

It was about 1900 hours when the big Army truck stopped. We were wide-eyed and in amazement as we climbed out of the back with our baggage and were instructed to wait in front of this great looking building. It was three stories high, made of cut stone with many large windows, and it was at least as long as a football field. The building was facing a large parking lot with row after row of Army Combat Vehicles. It reminded me of the Parliament buildings that I had seen pictures of in England on Downing Street. I could not believe this was going to be my new home, but I was not sure, so I did not even let my mind go there, as I did not want to be disappointed. I looked behind me, and on the other side of the area was the same type of building. The air was cool; a light jacket was all that we needed to stay warm. It just felt different—quite different—as we waited to see what was in store for us. This would be my first night in a foreign country. Frankfurt, Germany, had only been a place in the history books. Now I was living and walking down that historic road. I was—and still am—a blessed man.

A young Private First Class came and had us leave our duffel bags and handbags just inside the big doors of the first entryway. He said that the mess hall had stayed open for us and was waiting to serve us an evening meal. I just loved the way he said it: to serve us an *evening meal.* As we entered this large area, I was in awe at how inviting it looked inside. This was not the average mess hall that I had grown used too. We were assigned a table that had a very pretty cloth. One of the cooks came over and informed us that he had made a couple of different dishes for us. I was thinking, *is this real? Is this just an indoctrination, or what?* He invited us to come to the serving area, and I could not believe all the wonderful-looking and great-smelling food that had been prepared for us. I had just arrived, and now I would have re-enlisted there on the spot just for the food. This guy was friendly. He talked to us and welcomed us to the 3rd Quartermaster Battalion, Company B Transportation Company. It was too good to be true.

It seemed like we ate about three pounds of food each, because so much had been laid out there just for us. My mind wandered back to the two weeks on the Navy ship, which was not yet twelve hours behind me, and that experience was already a fading memory. I know the Navy is a great organization, and I also know that most of Navy life is very good. During my life, I have met some great people, who had served many years on the high seas, and they loved it, but for me, I was in my glory having just arrived in Deutschland, with my feet on solid ground. The first impression was one of amazement. *Why me, Lord?*

After we had had our fill, we were taken back to where we had left our bags and then to a room that was set up for just six people, almost like a hotel room. My friend Mitchell was sent to the second floor. I was assigned to another company on the first floor area. Two other GIs and I were in the same room, with three fellows who had been there for a few months. We were the newbie's.

I could see that the wall locker that we hung our clothes in was twice as large as I was used too. The floors were reddish hardwood and waxed to a high shine. The bathroom had enclosed single stalls. *Wow! How much more of this is there?* Our bunks were single beds, not stacked two high or five high like the Navy. Clean sheets and blankets were already there. All we had to do was shower and then call it a day. I was so tired but so excited that I did not want to succumb to sleep.

We sat on our footlockers and talked until we were told to turn out the lights. There was a lot of processing to be completed the next day. Here I was in a place where a great war had been fought, living in the very barracks that the German soldiers had lived in, on a different continent, a different world, among people who spoke a different language. I had to pinch myself to make sure that I was not dreaming.

It seemed as if I had just gone to sleep and now they were waking us up. I must have just closed my eyes and just passed out. It was now morning, and we were told where to go to stand in formation and meet the rest of our platoon. Then we went back to this wonderful place to have breakfast. Now, the mess hall area was completely full; hundreds of soldiers were there and still more standing in line. The cook asked me how I wanted my eggs. *How did I want my eggs?* That was a first for me. Usually they just threw everything on our trays and we ate whatever had been served to us. It seemed like there must have been a hundred different items to choose from, as we moved through the chow line. If all this was real, then I had definitely made the right choice about which service to join. After the cruise across the big pond, I weighed only one hundred, forty pounds, and my clothes were a loose fit. I did not like that. At six-foot-one I needed to put on some weight, and after just having two meals in that mess hall, there was hope.

Here we were in Europe; the Cold War was at its peak. The Berlin Wall was only a day's ride from where we were. I was almost on the front line, and I thought, if the Russians came across the border, we would be looking them in the eye in a matter of hours.

The first few days were what the Army called "in processing." After a wonderful breakfast, we went to our rooms and got everything all ready for the day. We always had to have everything in order, because we never knew when there would be a surprise walk-through inspection. We were introduced to our Platoon Sergeant. Sergeant First Class Holly was a strict, no-nonsense type; yet, as time went on, I found that he was easy to get along with. If you just did things his way, you would be at the top of his good list. He liked things pretty near perfect; he liked those who liked the Army, those who had a good attitude, and those who wanted to be the best. He was my kind of a person.

The Third Armored Division Headquarters was just across the cobblestone street in an area called Drake. My area was called Edwards. Most of the time, it was called Drake-Edwards Kerosene. That was where the division personnel office was, and we all had to go over there for a records check and to make sure everything was in order.

The fellow who was checking my records wanted to know what my Social Security number was. I said, "I don't know."

"What you mean you don't know?" He said.

I looked at him and thought *what the heck he is talking about?* I had never heard of Social Security before, and if I had a number with that name, I sure didn't know it. He could not believe it. The paperwork was completed, and now I had a new number to memorize, along with my Army serial number and my rifle number.

Sergeant Holly had us all get refitted with new clothes, combat boots, and dress shoes. Now, all my uniforms were a much better fit, and I liked that. We were issued winter clothing, coats, and winter shoes called "Mickey Mouse Boots." They kept our feet nice and warm. Now I knew why the wall locker was twice as big as the ones at Fort Hood—we had twice as much clothing. We had a few days of classes, mostly about life in Germany and about being prepared if a conflict broke out…in other words, war. This was serious business. It was a must that we knew what to do and what our duties were. So much had to be accomplished in just a few minutes. Then we went through a practice dry run, and of course, we didn't do it right and not nearly fast enough. We practiced until we got it right. It had to be right. Sergeant Holly would not accept anything less than a perfect performance.

We were assigned a vehicle to drive. I was assigned my very own five-ton combat Army truck. The bumper number was B-114. I looked at it and thought it was one heck of a big truck. It had a canvas top cab, a large canvas cover over the back, and it could transport twenty to thirty fully-equipped combat troops. I stood there and just looked at it. Then I walked around and admired the size of that monster. I almost needed a ladder to climb into the cab. It even smelled good. The smell of the Army Green Canvas was a kind of a manly smell, I thought. What a truck, and now it was mine to drive—my responsibility to keep clean, in good running order, and as Sergeant Holly said, ready to go at a moment's notice.

Later that day, I had some free time and went back out to where number 114 was parked, just to climb into it and sit there in total amazement. Only a few months back, I was following a mule, looking at its south end while going northbound. Sergeant Holly saw me and came by to see what I was doing. He was impressed that I was impressed.

The next few days were spent taking my truck for short runs with an experienced driver sitting in the right seat. I passed all the driving tests and went back to the classroom for more instruction on the German rules of the road. We had to know how to read the road signs, know where we were, convert miles per hour to kilometers, and a hundred other foreign things. I was definitely not driving a team of mules, pulling a steel-tired farm wagon down a dusty county road in Alabama. I was in a different world and was riding high, wishing that Conley could see me now. I think he would have been proud of me.

For the most part, I was always in total amazement, thinking all this couldn't be real. I really had it made. The Army life was right down my lane; I loved the dress-right-dress and having everything all lined up. It was easy for me to be one of the best. My attitude was that someone had to be the very best...why not me? Everything, every day was exciting. I knew what was expected of me, and just for the heck of it, I gave much more than was expected. Now, I am not bragging. It was easy for me to do this; it was my thing. It was so easy to make my shoes shinier than everyone else's, and it only took a few more minutes to do that.

Each evening, we were notified where we would be driving the next day. One day, it was delivering rations to other units forty to fifty kilometers away. The next day, we were hauling mail, and the next, picking up troops that had been on training missions. In a matter of weeks, I had been dispatched to many different places delivering all kinds of materials to units in and around the Frankfurt area.

I washed and cleaned my truck every day, even if I had not driven it. That wasn't hard and not much to brag about, but it was something I wanted to do. Sergeant Holly was watching me, and that made me want to do even more. I think it is a good thing to impress your teacher, your boss, your coach, and your sergeant.

The Post Exchange was just across the street at Drake. Each month, as we got paid in cash, we all made a trip over to the PX to get things we needed and just look at all the items there in that big store. For me, it was nice to go get something new. Now, here you might think I was a little weird. Maybe I was. Maybe I still am, but just buying a new toothbrush that was a different color than the one I had or a different kind of toothpaste, or different smelling hand soap gave me a thrill. Maybe I'd get a new towel...a real one, or one of a hundred different items that were sold there. That was a privilege I had never had before. It was even more exciting just to bring it back to my room and lay it all out there on my bunk and just look at it, to smell it, to admire all that I had. I was a rich man—a really rich man. I always did that and still do to this day. When I buy something, I bring it home and just enjoy looking at it and putting it away all lined up in the closet or cupboards.

The one little thing that got to me there in my new home was an early-morning wake-up around 0400. This happened about once a month for the first year or so. The Army medics would make a trip through the barracks, checking each soldier for venereal disease. Most of us never got used to this, but it was a sight to see the first time it happened. Well, maybe a sight most people wouldn't want to see.

We never knew when this would happen. It was called a "short-arms inspection." (I know, I know but that is what they called it) Two or three medics would come into our room unannounced, turn on the lights, and wake everyone up. Then they'd have us stand there by our bunks in our shorts. There were three of us on each side of the room.

We were still half-asleep, and nobody was smiling. I was the first bunk on the left and, therefore, the first one to be inspected. The medic said to me, "Let's have a look," as he turned on his Army flashlight and pointed at my Army-issued shorts. I thought *Okay...look at what?*

Now, remember, this was the very first time for me. He said, "Drop your shorts." *Does he want to check my drawers? Why would he want to check them?* I pulled down my shorts and just stood there looking very embarrassed. I don't want to go into all the details, but I had no idea what he was trying to tell me to do. My roommates across the room were looking at me with grins on their faces, while I started to sweat, trying to follow the medic's instructions. I didn't think it was the least bit funny. I had no idea what he wanted me to do, so he went to the next guy and told me to watch, as he inspected him. I did *not* want to see *that.* I did not want to be looking at some ugly GI with his shorts down to his knees. I knew then that the rest of the guys were smiling, because they knew I was not the smartest guy on the block.

Anyway, I finally figured out want they wanted me to do, and they were gone. Now, I had to face the other five in my room as they gave me a hard time and were laughing at me about how to do a short-arms inspection. For sure, they all knew I was a country hick and dumber than a rock. I never got used to this and was so glad that they discontinued this kind of inspection later on. Sergeant Holly would embarrass me from time to time when we were all together, and the whole platoon would have a good laugh at me, as he tried to get me to show him how a short-arms inspection should be preformed. Everyone thought it was so funny...except yours truly.

I was growing up fast, learning the ways of the world, loving the Army life. By now, I was at the Army Education Center twice a week from 1900 hours to 2100 hours, taking classes so that I could pass my GED test. My plans were to enroll in college as soon as I completed all that. The Army encouraged those who wanted to continue their education, but it had to be in the evening. I passed with really good scores and was back in class the very next week, taking college courses that were provided through the University of Maryland. I continued those for the next twenty years. It was almost a free college education with some great instructors. Some courses were done through correspondence. It was hard, knowing that my buddies were out having fun, while I was cooped up in a study hall or classroom. There were times I really had to give myself a pep talk....It wasn't easy.

By now, I had pretty much made up my mind that this was going to be my career. For me, it was the right thing to do; there were not many other options. The Army life is not for everyone, and that is a good thing. I have always wanted to be the best or at least one of the best, and the Army provided that opportunity for anyone who wanted to take that path. It was an easy decision for me to make.

Later on, I received a letter from my mom, informing me that there was a new baby boy at their house. John Dolan was the new addition to our family, and it was wonderful news from back home. I could not wait to see him. Also, my parents were moving...to a new address. Rural Route One would not be my permanent address anymore.

Well, this is my little story from the hills of Alabama—a real know-nothing country boy being accepted as a soldier in the United States Army. I never looked back, and I would not trade any part of my life with any other person. Being born and raised on Rural Route One was a gift that I have come to appreciate more and more as I grow older. I love where I came from and where I am today. I believe anyone who tries can do whatever he or she wants.

Chapter 18

Looking Back

The lessons I learned while growing up on "Rural Route One" have been useful in almost every aspect of my life, even to this day. I was born at the most wonderful time into a wonderful family in a wonderful country. I never considered myself poor, over-worked, deprived, or mistreated. Life was just different there on that dusty country road. Living there in a most beautiful part of the world is forever stamped on my mind. There on rural route, I learned about life.

It was so important for all of us to know what the main thing is, that we were all in this together. That we all had to pull and push the wagon, that there were no free rides. All of us worked, all of us sat down at the same table; no one was treated any better than the other. I thought that was fair.

We all had to work to survive; it took all of us working together, as a family, to make it. Everyone had to hoe cotton; everyone had to pick cotton and pull the pick sack. There were no welfare programs, no food stamps, and no unemployment for us to fall back on. It was just plain old-fashioned work that kept the food on our table. We worked from sunup to sundown, using every hour of the day to keep the farm going. No one sat in the shade, while someone else worked. Working as a family/team, so much more can be accomplished.

A dollar was hard to come by. I worked for three dollars a day and, at that time, I was proud to get the work. We all learned at a very young age the value of money. My dad handled the finances; there were no checkbooks, no bank accounts, and no savings account. Later, when I was hired out to work, he collected the pay. The money I made helped with things we needed as a family. He controlled the spending from his billfold there in his blue-denim farm overalls. If you wanted a dollar you had to go to him. Also, I learned that even though I made more money, I could not have more than my other siblings. Of course, I was selfish and did not like that, but it was the right thing. I had to do without so that we all could be equal… a good lesson to learn, for sure. It is good that only one person in the household kept tabs on the purse. Too many fingers in the till causes it to go broke. Accountability was the lifeblood of the income for survival.

There I learned that life is not always fair. I thought that I needed things, and I wanted things, and I had to do without things. With that many brothers and sisters, we had to share and share alike, not one of us was any more special than the other. My friends had nicer and better things. I really wanted to fit in and be like them, but that was not to be. For me, this was the hardest of all lessons to learn. The parents hardly ever understand peer pressure, because each generation is different.

It is OK to look back to see where you came from, to learn from past mistakes, and profit from them. And, my goodness, it is a wonderful thing to dream, to look forward; it is good to better oneself in life, to always leave things better than what you found them. Each of us is different, and we have to find our own way. Trying to find just the right career, the right job, the right location to live was exciting for me. Living on that dusty road caused me to reflect on where I wanted to go in life. Life is to be lived at its fullest. I knew that living as a sharecroppers son was not my thing. Yet, growing up on "Rural Route One" gave me strength to go forward to see what was over the next hill. I also learned that if the grass is greener on the other side, the water bill is higher. I now knew how to work, how to work as a team, how to save, and I learned that dreams really do come true.

The world has so much to offer, the opportunities numerous and unlimited; they always have been and always will be, even to this day. I understood at a very young age to keep looking forward. There are people out there just waiting to help...but you have to find them and ask. Teachers, coaches, and friends all want you to succeed in life. Doors are there just waiting to be opened.

I learned that it is not always easy, life gets in the way, mistakes are made, wrong choices, bad decisions and, at times, being just plain stupid will keep you down for a while—but not for long. I knew how to get back up, dust myself off, and get back in the race. I knew that, even though I had nothing tangible, I was more blessed than most people were. For me, being raised poor was an asset.

Life has been very good to me and still is. I was fortunate to have grown up in Morgan County on "Rural Route One." Joppa, Alabama

I am among all men most richly blessed.

William McDaniel McCollum

All my brothers and sisters still lives very close to where we were raised there in Morgan County, Alabama

Conley is about ready to retire and do some serious fishing I think. God only made one of him; he is the best brother anyone could ever dream of having.

Lena Elizabeth is enjoying the retirement life style now. She worked most of her life and had fun serving others as a waitress. She is wonderful person, a special sister for sure.

Francis, my buddy grew up to be a really good musician with a wonderful voice. She and her husband have traveled all over the south performing. What a great lady she is.

Wanda is also enjoying life; she has always been a wonderful sister. She loves people, loves the little things of life, and she loves Elvis.

Thomas Randolph wanted so much to be a preacher. He died in a truck accident in 2008. What a loss, he is truly missed by all of us.

Juanita "Nita" has so much talent, and is so much fun to be with. She is the rocket scientist in our family and a really great lady.

Rachel has dedicated her life to serving others. First as a nurse and now a school teacher, we are so blessed to have her as our little sister.

John Dolan my little brother. John enjoys life, likes the great outdoors and works really hard at being the best truck driver that has ever driven an eighteen wheeler.

Our mom died in 1992 at the age of 73. Dad passed away in 1997 at the age of 85. Both are buried at Walnut Grove Baptist Church, Morgan County, Alabama.

9883988R0007

Made in the USA
Charleston, SC
21 October 2011